Fred Farrokh's *Prepare for*
readers an essential and
suffering and devotion of the early church. Farrokh's clear and
concise style and faithfulness to the biblical text combine to
create a fresh, new perspective that captures the heart of the
people of the Way, and it models a commitment to Christ for the
contemporary church.

—**Rev. Robert L. Gallagher, PhD**
Professor Emeritus of Intercultural Studies,
Wheaton College Graduate School
Author of *Mission in Acts:*
Ancient Narratives in Contemporary Contexts

In this book, Fred Farrokh mines the Acts of the Apostles for
practical lessons for the global church today in relation to the
growing reality of persecution. Drawing on over three decades
of ministry praxis, his own experience as an Iranian convert
from Islam, and an academically-informed understanding of the
historical and cultural context of the Scriptures, he presents to us
lessons that are at once realistic, pastoral, and applicable.

—**Duane Alexander Miller, PhD**
Priest at the Anglican Cathedral of the Redeemer,
associate professor at the Protestant Faculty of Theology at Madrid
(UEBE), and author of *Two Stories of Everything:*
The Competing Metanarratives of Islam and Christianity

Prepare for Persecution: Lessons from Acts is a gift for our times.
Dr. Farrokh has provided us with a fresh perspective on the book
of Acts. He leads us on a journey of discovery in our study of the
Bible. This opens up a neglected view of God's Word to us. The
experience addresses the world today in a most timely way, along
with some excellent analysis and valuable insights. I recommend
we all read this book and take it to heart.

—**Mike Webster, DMin**
Director, Redeemer School of Ministry
President Emeritus, Elim Bible Institute and College

PREPARE *for* PERSECUTION

FRED FARROKH

PREPARE *for* PERSECUTION

Lessons from Acts

CONTENTS

Foreword 1

Introduction 5

Chapter 1: *An Overcoming Church* 13

Chapter 2: *The Acts of the Holy Spirit* 37

Chapter 3: *The Bible Students* 49

Chapter 4: *Solomon's Portico* 63

Chapter 5: *Honestly!* 75

Chapter 6: *From Persecutor to Apostle* 87

Chapter 7: *A Gospel for the Gentiles* 97

Chapter 8: *Misrepresented!* 109

Chapter 9: *Legal Trials* 121

Conclusion: *The Power of an Indestructible Life* 137

Acknowledgments 140

Endnotes 141

FOREWORD

In solemn words of warning reported in all four Gospels, Jesus spoke to His followers of the persecutions to come. Like master, like servant: "'A slave is not greater than his master.' If they persecuted Me, they will persecute you" (John 15:20). These persecutions were to be no random, sporadic, or light thing. The warning was clear and sobering, "They will hand you over to tribulation and kill you, and you will be hated by all nations because of My name" (Matthew 24:9).

Through what lens do you view history? A standard perspective offered in the West is that we are all experiencing a process of steady moral and material improvements. This is called "progress." This comforting message is served up to us despite all evidence to the contrary. Yet this was not how Jesus saw the future course of history, not for His church. The future for believers, Jesus warned, will be marked by rejection, trials, and persecution.

There will be gospel advance, to be sure, to the ends of the earth until He returns, but along with this, there will be steady, persistent, targeted, violent opposition to the truth. As we read the pages of the Gospels, we can see that, in many ways, through direct teaching and parables, Jesus was preparing His church to endure suffering. "Rejoice and be glad," He said, when people persecute you, for you will be in the best of company.

But are we truly ready? And if not, can we be teachable? For decades now, prophetic voices have been warning the Western church to ready itself for the trials to come. As the faith of many has grown cold, those who hold fast have been urged to focus their eyes on the One who can guide them through the coming storms. These warnings have come from diverse places. Some have been Christian witnesses whose faith survived under the Iron Curtain but who now sense the shutters closing over truth in the West. Other calls have come from those who have dedicated themselves to loving and nurturing the persecuted church.

In this timely and strategic book, a "Get ready" warning has been issued by a precious Christian brother, Dr. Fred Farrokh, who was born in the House of Islam and reborn into Jesus' family. He is no stranger to the hatred of the cross, and with an outsider's fresh eyes, he yearned to equip his brothers and sisters to be ready to stand their ground.

To be kingdom-ready, it is not enough to be entertained by novel ideas. We need to be consumers and appliers of the Word, not just onlookers to it. One of God's great and most powerful tools for feeding on the Word of Life is the gathered fellowship, in which a group of believers gathers around the Scriptures, to be fed, strengthened, and equipped to live well. This is an indispensable key to standing firm in troubled times.

What a great gift this book is to all such groups. While it can and will be read with great profit by many individuals, it will surely be a powerful resource to unite earnest seekers after truth, as they come together to profit from the extraordinary Acts of the Apostles.

Dr. Mark Durie
Senior Research Fellow, Melbourne School of Theology,
Director of the Institute for Spiritual Awareness

INTRODUCTION

For behold, darkness will cover the earth
And deep darkness the peoples;
But the LORD will rise upon you
And His glory will appear upon you.
Nations will come to your light,
And kings to the brightness of your rising. —Isaiah 60:2–3

At the beginning of the third decade of the third millennium, we look around and see that darkness is covering the earth. In areas and pockets, deep darkness has covered the peoples. Evil is being unleashed to challenge the body of Christ. Are you ready? How will you respond?

The good news is that we have not been left helpless. When we open our Bibles, we find reports of persecution on almost every page of the Acts of the Apostles. There we also find the distilled wisdom of the early church, which was able to overcome persecution and flourish through it. So let us go on a journey with the early Christians in the book of Acts, gleaning valuable lessons from them and drawing strength from their overcoming spirit.

Today the body of Christ faces many challenges. We have heard of the persecution of Christians and churches in Muslim and Communist lands. This continues. At the same time, a dark cloud of opposition and persecution—an anti-Christ spirit—appears to be spreading even now in the Western world. In "free" countries, some Christians are even meeting in underground churches or home groups to avoid governmental interference. The coronavirus pandemic has provided a cover for ungodly leaders to entangle churches with restrictive regulations. It is true that Europe and North America have strong Christian foundations, but those foundations are being denied, eroded, and even destroyed. As an example, the European Union rejected any mention of Christianity in its recent foundational constitution.

The West has been overcome with the "Nebuchadnezzar Syndrome"—losing faith in God and then losing your mind. Nebuchadnezzar, the great emperor of Babylon held the Jewish boys Daniel, Shadrach, Meshach, and Abed-Nego as his captives. As they witnessed to him of the one true God, he grew more and more proud. Refusing to repent, he persecuted his God-fearing servants by tossing them into the flames. So God said, "Let his mind change from that of a human. And let an animal's mind be given to him . . . until you [Nebuchadnezzar] recognize that the Most High is ruler over the realm of mankind and bestows it on whomever He wishes" (Daniel 4:16, 32). First, the great emperor rejected the one true God, then he lost his mind. So it is today.

Praise God that Nebuchadnezzar eventually repented and glorified God. Then his sanity was restored. So, there is hope for nations today because of the great mercy of God.

A Note on Persecution

The Cambridge Dictionary defines persecution as "unfair or cruel treatment over a long period of time because of race, religion, or political beliefs." [1] The etymology of persecution stems from "pursuing" with hostility.

Several questions persist. Is the entire church persecuted, always and at all times? If so, is "the persecuted church" merely a synonym for "the church"? And, if so, does this mitigate the difference between severe persecution, in which believers "did not love their life, even when faced with death" (Revelation 12:11), and less severe forms of persecution, particularly in countries noted for religious freedom? Certainly, different types and levels of persecution exist. Chapter 1 considers each of these.

Ajith Fernando of Sri Lanka has written an excellent commentary on Acts from his Asian perspective. He gives special emphasis to the theme of persecution: "After chapter 3 only three chapters in Acts do not mention persecution. This suggests that persecution may be a necessary part of the Christian life." [2]

Rejecting Victimhood Status

The Holy Spirit's emphasis in Acts is on overcoming persecution, not on embracing a state of permanent victimization. In many Western nations, many people earnestly seek to claim the mantle of victimhood. Generally, people in Eastern cultures carry no comparable aspiration, since victimhood is equated with shame and lowliness. In the West, however, victimization has become a political force demanding compensation and reparation.

A persecuted church is not a disabled church. A joke has circulated about three men walking down the street. They see a bearded man coming toward them on the street. In hushed tones they ask each other, "Isn't that Jesus?" Indeed, it is Jesus. As Jesus approaches, the first says to Jesus, "Lord Jesus, I have terrible back pain." Jesus immediately lays hands on the man and heals him. The second says, "Jesus, my shoulder is injured." He demonstrates that he cannot lift his arm above his head. Jesus likewise immediately heals him. Right away, the third man yells out, "Jesus, don't touch me, I'm receiving disability payments!"

As this illustration depicts, there are some benefits in the West to being a victim. It may pay. The downside of this reality is that it may create ulterior motives for becoming a victim. Hence, it may become difficult to distinguish between those who are legitimately disabled and those who are outright faking.

Victimhood is similar in some ways to disability. Many people are victims, injured severely by the sins of others. History is a butcher's bench, according to Hegel. People and people groups need to experience healing and reconciliation to move forward in wholeness.

Unfortunately, in the new calculus of victimization, victims can thereafter do no wrong. Victims stand absolved from the consequences of their actions. If they burn down cities in protest, many will rationalize these actions as justifiable.

Such a mindset must be rejected. The Bible does not justify retaliation or revenge. Individuals and groups are responsible for their words and actions. Two wrongs do not make a right. While we should have compassion, as Jesus did, for those trampled upon by life, we should not join the rush to claim the mantle of victimization to absolve ourselves of the consequences of our own sins. We should not seek to ply others for pity.

In the Acts of the Apostles, we do not see a group of complainers or permanent victims. Instead, we see overcomers who believe in the Lord Jesus. Christ's disciples are fortified by the Holy Spirit, who enables them to overcome every obstacle. They grow stronger through trials and tribulations. They overcome persecution through faith and perseverance. The early church would ultimately outshine and outlast the disbelief held by a subset of the Jewish religious leadership. They would likewise eclipse the Greco-Roman paganism and emperor worship that ruled the expanding milieu of Christ's church. The early church was a triumphant church.

The Genesis of Acts

Acts parallels Genesis in several ways. Genesis begins with a universal history of creation. The narrative continues to the fall of Adam and Eve, Noah's flood, and then the Tower of Babel. In Genesis 12, the universal focus immediately narrows to a focus on Abraham and his descendants. That narrow focus continues through to the end of Genesis, concluding with the death of Jacob and the blessing of the sons of Israel.

Regarding Acts, the early church was one community, initially located in Jerusalem. No denominations or branches existed. In fact, the church was initially composed solely of Messianic Jews who would later bring Gentiles into their movement. Judaism would eventually split between this Messianic Judaism based on Messiah Jesus, and a Rabbinic Judaism that concluded that Jesus of Nazareth was not the awaited messiah.

Luke chronicles the story of that early Jewish church by writing the Acts of the Apostles. The key figures were Jesus' twelve disciples. Jesus' inner circle of Peter, James, and John feature prominently in Acts. Other leaders emerge, such as Stephen, Philip, and James the brother of Jesus. Beginning with

Acts 9, and then fully by Acts 13, the focus of Acts becomes the work of God surrounding the life and ministry of the apostle Paul. Paul had been known as Saul, a fierce persecutor of the church. Through many narratives using "we" terminology, Luke indicates he was a traveling companion of Paul. Thus, he could write about those events in precise detail.

Though Acts, like Genesis, concludes with a narrow focus, we cannot discount the contributions of the other apostles to the growth of the early church. All the remaining original disciples, including Thomas, Matthew, Andrew, and Bartholomew, are recorded in church history as having had profound ministries. Thomas is reputed to have traveled the furthest to witness of his Lord Jesus, ultimately become a martyr in India. The church he planted in India remains steadfast to this day.

One reason the Holy Spirit may have inspired Luke to focus the latter half of Acts on Paul's ministry is the trials and legal entanglements faced by Paul. These multiple trials may appear a bit repetitive and even boring compared with the riveting missionary travels described immediately prior to them. However, the worldwide persecuted church has drawn both inspiration and insight from Paul, the persecutor who became an apostle, and then a prisoner. From Paul's arrival in Jerusalem late in Acts 21, through to the end of Acts 28, Paul is a prisoner.

The Holy Spirit has provided encouragement and insight to the persecuted church of Christ across the ages by featuring Paul in chains. The church of Christ today will be encouraged by a fresh look at our earliest family history. May the Lord Jesus Christ be glorified.

The Storylines of Acts

Like all books of the Bible, the Acts of the Apostles contains many inspirational themes and storylines. How the early church overcame persecution and continued witnessing for Christ comprises one such theme. I have devoted one chapter to each storyline or theme. Each chapter concludes with a "For Further Discussion" section that may be utilized by individuals or Bible study groups.

Acts features at least nine critical storylines. Still others could have been selected, such as: miracles; angelic visitations; and the theological emphases of the early church. Each of these themes, as well as others, are sprinkled through the storylines I have selected. This book is not an in-depth commentary, but something more of an uplifting devotional, based on these storylines. These stories and histories, with their chapter numbers, are:

1. An Overcoming Church
2. The Acts of the Holy Spirit
3. The Bible Students
4. Solomon's Portico
5. Honestly!
6. From Persecutor to Apostle
7. A Gospel for the Gentiles
8. Misrepresented!
9. Legal Trials

Our study concludes with a final chapter, on the Indestructible Life that is found uniquely in our Lord Jesus Christ. Indeed, Jesus provides abundant life for believers today, as well as eternal life in his presence for eternity.

The church is a family. The body of Christ is a community. The book of Acts describes the beginning of our family history. Acts comprises the second part of Luke's two-part series that includes the Gospel of Luke and the Acts of the Apostles. Acts narrates approximately 30 years—the first three decades of the life of the early church after the resurrection of the Lord Jesus Christ. Let us begin.

CHAPTER 1

AN OVERCOMING CHURCH

The theme of the church of Jesus Christ overcoming persecution continues uninterrupted throughout the Acts of the Apostles. Luke continues this theme from his gospel, in which Jesus was brutally crucified, but then wondrously rises from the dead. After the ascension of the Lord, his disciples found themselves in hostile and somewhat unfamiliar territory. They must have wondered if they would soon become martyrs.

In Acts, we see the following forms of persecution arise, noted with their initial or primary reference:

- Mocking (Acts 2)
- Arrest (Acts 4)
- Threats (Acts 4)
- Imprisonment (Acts 4–5)
- Physical Assaults (Acts 5)
- Martyrdom (Acts 6, 12)
- Expulsion (Acts 9, 13)
- Legal Entanglements (Acts 21–28)

The Holy Spirit helped the disciples of Jesus overcome every type of persecution. Through these trials, their faith in Jesus grew and they rejoiced often. And the kingdom of God continued to expand. Acts does not present a shallow triumphalism, in which challenges are glossed over. In fact, Acts presents with truth and precision the challenges faced by the early church.

It is Christ in the Church Who is Being Persecuted

The conversion of Saul of Tarsus in Acts 9 provides a key to understanding the persecution of Christians and the church. Saul, enraged by Stephen's testimony and emboldened by the apparent ease with which Stephen's opponents were able to martyr him, set out to do the same to other followers of the Way:

> *Now as he was traveling, it happened that he was approaching Damascus, and suddenly a light from heaven flashed around him; and he fell to the ground and heard a voice saying to him, "Saul, Saul, why are you persecuting Me?" And he said, "Who are You, Lord?" And He said, "I am Jesus whom you are persecuting."*
> —Acts 9:3–5

Simply stated, Saul was persecuting Jesus who is present in the church. That same spirit has been present in the persecution of Christians from that time until now.

Mocking and Jeering on the Day of Pentecost

Acts 1 describes the disciples huddled in an upper room in Jerusalem (v. 13). It seems they were a bit unsure what to do next. They knew what befell Jesus in that same city. But the Day of Pentecost transformed the atmosphere. The Holy Spirit breathed life, purpose, and power into the church. So many souls were saved that day that the church became a growing movement.

When the Holy Spirit fell on the disciples in Acts 2, the onlookers did not know how to interpret what was happening.

> *Now there were Jews residing in Jerusalem, devout men from every nation under heaven. And when this sound occurred, the crowd came together and they were bewildered, because each one of them was hearing them speak in his own language . . . But others were jeering and saying, "They are full of sweet wine!"* —Acts 2:5–6, 13

The "jeering" described in 2:13 can be translated as "mock, deride, or jeer" according to *The Blue Letter Bible*.[3] The verb is also used in Acts 17:32, regarding the Athenians' response to Paul's preaching. Though mocking, jeering, or making fun of seems to pale in comparison to physical persecution, such as killing people, mocking should not be ignored or excused. This mocking and jeering sought to discourage the work of God. People may become disheartened or discouraged after being mocked. Those who jeer seek to shame, embarrass, or marginalize. Mocking can be the first stage of a slippery slope toward more severe forms of persecution. Those who are mocked may become fearful and unwilling to fully participate in public life.

In the West today, a creeping form of this type of persecution has arisen. Christian views and biblical views are derided and jeered. This sentiment holds sway particularly in the elitist circles of academia and media, creating a suffocating environment with limited freedom of expression. This derision is often accompanied by threats, which shall be explored below.

In the Old Testament, Nehemiah narrated a similar situation in which adversaries to the work of God used mocking to try to stop the work of God.

> *Now it came about that when Sanballat heard that we were rebuilding the wall, he became furious and very angry, and he mocked the Jews. And he spoke in the presence of his brothers and the wealthy people of Samaria and said, "What are these feeble Jews doing? Are they going to restore the temple for themselves? Can they offer sacrifices? Can they finish it in a day? Can they revive the stones from the heaps of rubble, even the burned ones?" Now Tobiah the Ammonite was near him, and he said, "Even what they are building—if a fox were to jump on it, it would break their stone wall down!"* —Nehemiah 4:1–3

Sanballat mocked the Jews and ridiculed the work of God. He had one purpose in mind: to dishearten God's people so they would stop the work of building the wall. Nehemiah wisely saw through Sanballat's evil plan. He prayed to God, encouraged his brethren, and continued the work through to its completion. He did not stop the work God had called him to do.

In Acts 2, the disciples faced a similar challenge. They were mocked—even as the Holy Spirit was being poured out. The very thing God was doing was being mocked by the scornful. David warns us not to sit in the seat of scoffers (Psalm 1:1).

Persecution became a stepping-stone to victory, though, through the prompt action of Peter. Fifty days previously, Peter sat in a cloud of shame, weeping bitterly that he had denied his Lord. At Pentecost, Peter took his stand and interpreted what was happening. The fear of marginalization was replaced by a sense of fulfillment as Peter the Rock interpreted Old Testament scriptures. Instead of cowering in a defensive posture, Peter interpreted what was happening during this Pentecostal outpouring. He then pivoted forward into an altar call. Three thousand people repented, embraced Christ, and were added to the church.

Arrests and Threats at the Temple

The great momentum of Pentecost continued in Acts 3 with the healing of the lame man at the Beautiful Gate. Peter wisely followed up the healing by preaching the gospel. The disciples did not need to wait long for persecution to strike again. Acts 4 begins with the arrest of Peter and John:

> As they were speaking to the people, the priests and the captain of the temple guard and the Sadducees came up to them, being greatly disturbed because they were teaching the people and proclaiming in Jesus the resurrection from the dead. And they laid hands on them and put them in prison until the next day, for it was already evening. But many of those who had heard the message believed; and the number of the men came to be about five thousand. —Acts 4:1-4

The main subset of Jewish religious leadership opposed Christ. They would later oppose Christ's apostles. To be clear, this was not a Jewish versus Christian issue. All the players in the drama, save for the Romans involved, were Jewish. The heroes of the New Testament story, including the Virgin Mary, Zechariah, Elisabeth, John the Baptist, the disciples, and Jesus himself, were Jewish. Some of the Jewish religious leaders, such as Nicodemus and Joseph of Arimathea, would themselves become disciples of Christ. So, it can be summarized that some of the Jewish religious leadership embraced Christ, while most opposed him.

The oppositional Jewish religious leaders conferred about how to handle the disciples of Christ. Their strategy came to include a different type of persecution—threats:

> And when they had summoned them, they commanded them not to speak or teach at all in the name of Jesus. But Peter and John answered and said to them, "Whether it is right in the sight of God to listen to you rather than to God, make your own judgment; for we cannot stop speaking about what we have seen and heard." When they had threatened them further, they let them go (finding no basis on which to punish them) on account of the people, because they were all glorifying God for what had happened. —Acts 4:18–21

Threats, like mocking, were an attempt to stop the work of God. The work of God was evangelism; these Jewish religious leaders forbade these messianic Jewish apostles "to speak or teach at all in the name of Jesus."

The Holy Spirit again overcame this persecution in and through the lives of the disciples of Jesus. The disciples did not shrink back in fear, which is what the devil seeks to accomplish when he incites people to persecute Christians. Instead, the early believers prayed. The result was a fresh move of the Holy Spirit and the believers being filled with boldness: "And when they had prayed, the place where they had gathered together was shaken, and they were all filled with the Holy Spirit and began to speak the word of God with boldness" (Acts 4:31).

In this crisis period, the apostles could have shrunk back in fear. However, the Holy Spirit filled them with courage. And God's work continued.

Imprisonment

Christians have a long history of being imprisoned. The first recorded instances of imprisonment in Acts occur in 4:3 (quoted above) and now in 5:18, continuing at the point to which the narrative has brought us. After the incident with Ananias and Sapphira, which will be considered later in this book, the apostles continued their public ministry. They were promptly arrested by the religious leadership.

Luke tells us in Acts 5:17 the reason for the arrest: the religious leaders were jealous of both the crowds and fame that were shifting to the apostles. These religious leaders, with their hearts far from God, projected the same jealousy they had of Jesus onto Jesus' apostles. Even Pilate knew these leaders handed Jesus over to them because of jealousy (Matthew 27:18; Mark 15:10). That this information rose all the way up to Pilate meant that this jealousy was no public secret. Jealousy ate away at these leaders such that they committed murder. They were about to do it again. What a tragedy. We must remain on guard so that jealousy does not take root in our hearts. None of us is forever immune from it. Anytime we compare ourselves to others, there is the threat that such a root may seek to take hold.

Next, these oppositional religious leaders arrested the apostles. The narrative continues: "But the high priest stood up, along with all his associates (that is the sect of the Sadducees), and they were filled with jealousy. They laid hands on the apostles and put them in a public prison" (Acts 5:17–18).

Right from the beginning of church history, Christians have been arrested, detained, and imprisoned for their faith. Like Master, like servants. This occurrence would become common for the early church. The author of Hebrews writes: "Remember the prisoners, as though in prison with them, and those who are badly treated, since you yourselves also are in the body" (Hebrews 13:3). The history of the church has been a history of frequent imprisonment of its leaders. Let us pray for Christians who are imprisoned for the name of Jesus even today.

The imprisonment of the apostles in Acts 5:18 was not long-lasting:

> *But during the night an angel of the Lord opened the gates of the prison, and leading them out, he said, "Go, stand and speak to the people in the temple area the whole message of this Life." Upon hearing this, they entered into the temple area about daybreak and began to teach.* —Acts 5:19–21

Through his angel, God instructed the apostles to do the very thing that had gotten them imprisoned. This was God's defiant veto of the evil leadership of that day. The life-giving message of Jesus was more important in God's economy than the comfort of the disciples. They possessed a soul-saving message that needed to be preached.

God used the wisdom of Gamaliel to break the demonic momentum that could have led to the death of some of the apostles. Gamaliel wisely counseled his colleagues to take a wait-and-see approach. This advice was not easy for these leaders to accept. Even in the midst of persecution today, God may send help from unlikely sources. One of Gamaliel's students, Saul of

Tarsus, though not explicitly part of this Sanhedrin assembly, would later take a much more aggressive approach toward the disciples of Jesus than his teacher Gamaliel recommended.

Physical Assaults

The next type of persecution confronting the apostles was physical assault. Flogging was a common type of physical punishment used in New Testament times. Flogging meant to whip someone with lashes or beat them with rods. Jesus prophesied that his disciples would be flogged: "Therefore, behold, I am sending you prophets and wise men and scribes; some of them you will kill and crucify, and some of them you will flog in your synagogues, and persecute from city to city" (Matthew 23:34). Jesus himself was flogged at the time Pilate released Barabbas to the people (Matthew 27:26).

Even though Gamaliel's counsel softened the punishment that came to the apostles, they did not escape physical assaults. The religious leaders were angry because they could not scare the apostles into remaining silent about Christ. In a short sentence that should be in the hearts and on the lips of Christians today, Peter responded to additional threats with his famous statement: "We must obey God rather than men" (Acts 5:29). The oppositional religious leaders were not happy that they could not pressure Peter and his associates into silence. This meant the Jesus movement would thrive while the influence of this subset of religious leaders would continue to wane.

These religious leaders would manifest their anger toward the apostles by administering a painful flogging: "They followed his advice; and after calling the apostles in, they flogged them and ordered them not to speak in the name of Jesus, and then released them" (Acts 5:40).

In contemporary terms, these leaders were not interested in "freedom of religion." They sought to forbid the apostles from preaching Christ. They reinforced their threat with physical assaults—this time through whipping the apostles. In Christian history, imprisonment is often accompanied by physical assaults.

Amazingly, the narrative of Acts 5 ends not with discouragement but with encouragement!

> *So they went on their way from the presence of the Council, rejoicing that they had been considered worthy to suffer shame for His name. And every day, in the temple and from house to house, they did not stop teaching and preaching the good news of Jesus as the Christ.* —Acts 5:41–42

Even after a painful flogging, the disciples rejoiced. They had seen Jesus flogged. No doubt the Holy Spirit confirmed in their spirits that they were on the right track by following in Jesus' footsteps. Just as importantly, the apostles continued their ministry, both publicly and privately. The good news was being preached. The church was continuing to grow.

In our days, we can be encouraged even in the midst of persecution. We may be persecuted actively, or we may hear reports of believers in Christ being persecuted in other places. Jesus says there is a blessing that accompanies persecution:

> *Blessed are those who have been persecuted for the sake of righteousness, for theirs is the kingdom of heaven. Blessed are you when people insult you and persecute you, and falsely say all kinds of evil against you because*

*of Me. Rejoice and be glad, for your reward in heaven is
great; for in this same way they persecuted the prophets
who were before you.* —Matthew 5:10–12

Let us frequently pause to pray for all members of the body
of Christ enduring persecution. May their witness increase even
in the face of mocking, derision, imprisonment, and assaults.

More Assaults, More Imprisonments

Saul, as he ravaged the church, frequently had followers of
Christ thrown into prison (Acts 8:3). This was part of the "great
persecution" against the Jerusalem church (8:2). We will explore
the life of Saul more fully in the second half of this book. He
would later be imprisoned for Christ, so he was well aware of this
dynamic. The hunter would become the hunted. He would later
write to Timothy: "Indeed, all who want to live in a godly way in
Christ Jesus will be persecuted" (2 Timothy 3:12).

Paul and Barnabas would later lead what may be considered
the church's first missionary outreach, departing to Cyprus from
Antioch. During this trip, while preaching and working miracles
in Lystra, Paul and Barnabas were caught between the hammer of
pagan confusion and the anvil of Jewish physical persecution. When
God healed a lame man at Lystra, the Gentiles misattributed the
miracle to Zeus. Paul was ultimately able to correct this confusion.
Just when it seemed the apostles would enjoy a happy ending to
this ministry event, Jewish opponents to the work of God stoned
Paul to death. Or so these persecutors thought. Miraculously, God
used the prayers of a group of disciples to bring Paul back to life
(Acts 14:19–20).

In the Gentile environment of Macedonian Philippi, Paul and Silas encountered severe persecution accompanied by beatings and imprisonment:

> *The crowd joined in an attack against them, and the chief magistrates tore their robes off them and proceeded to order them to be beaten with rods. When they had struck them with many blows, they threw them into prison, commanding the jailer to guard them securely; and he, having received such a command, threw them into the inner prison and fastened their feet in the stocks.*
> —Acts 16:22–24

Paul and Silas must have been in intense physical pain, having been struck with many blows. Nothing about the prison experience was meant to comfort the prisoners. The Roman system was specifically meant to cause pain. Even the stocks were made to cut into the skin if the prisoner moved at all.

Paul and Silas responded in faith and worship. They sang praises to God, no doubt to buoy their own spirits, but also as a witness to the other prisoners. Music has always been a great instrument of evangelism. While they were singing, God set them free from prison. God also set the prison-keeper free from his sins.

> *Now about midnight Paul and Silas were praying and singing hymns of praise to God, and the prisoners were listening to them; and suddenly there was a great earthquake, so that the foundations of the prison were shaken; and immediately all the doors were opened, and everyone's chains were unfastened.* —Acts 16:25–26

Paul and Silas pivoted to bring the gospel to the Philippian jailer. The jailer, now relieved of his sins and the horrific prospect of letting the prisoners escape, washed the wounds of Paul and Silas. Otherwise, infection could have set in. There is a happy ending here but life in this type of prison was not easy or painless. Throughout Christian history, Christians have often found themselves in these types of situations. Throughout the world today, and increasingly in the West, Christians are being confronted by imprisonment for the decisions and actions flowing from their faith. For example, pastors are being arrested in places like the United States and Canada for refusing to effectively close their churches or severely limit attendance in the face of government "public health" commands. The debate centers on whether church services are "essential services."

Martyrdom: Stephen, the Church's First Martyr

Martyrdom is the most severe form of persecution. For believers, the martyr's crown awaits, which marks the conclusion of their ministry and witness on this earth.

Jesus tells the angel of the church of Smyrna: "Do not fear what you are about to suffer. Behold, the devil is about to throw some of you into prison, so that you will be tested, and you will have tribulation for ten days. Be faithful until death, and I will give you the crown of life" (Revelation 2:10).

Jesus in his revelation to John, also states that martyrs will have a special designation in the age to come:

When the Lamb broke the fifth seal, I saw underneath the altar the souls of those who had been killed because of the word of God, and because of the testimony which they had maintained; and they cried out with a loud

voice, saying, "How long, O Lord, holy and true, will
You refrain from judging and avenging our blood on
those who live on the earth?" And a white robe was
given to each of them; and they were told that they were
to rest for a little while longer, until the number of their
fellow servants and their brothers and sisters who were
to be killed even as they had been, was completed also.
—Revelation 6:9–11

Jesus esteems as precious the faith and steadfastness that results in a person laying down his or her life for him. Such commitment is a statement of worship of the King of Kings.

Martyrdom touched the early church through the life of Stephen. Stephen was one of the first set of deacons, a man of faith and fiery preaching. The martyrdom of Stephen was initiated by a different group, Jews living outside of Israel. Their strategy was eerily similar to that faced by Jesus. Matthew recounts:

Now the chief priests and the entire Council kept trying
to obtain false testimony against Jesus, so that they
might put Him to death. They did not find any, even
though many false witnesses came forward. But later on
two came forward, and said, "This man stated, 'I am
able to destroy the temple of God and to rebuild it in
three days.'" —Matthew 26:59–61

Several of the arguments used by Stephen's opponents were nearly verbatim to the false charges against Jesus. These accusations will resurface again in the allegations against Paul in Acts 21:21. Luke narrates in Acts 6:

And Stephen, full of grace and power, was performing great wonders and signs among the people. But some men from what was called the Synagogue of the Freedmen, including both Cyrenians and Alexandrians, and some from Cilicia and Asia, rose up and argued with Stephen. But they were unable to cope with his wisdom and the Spirit by whom he was speaking. Then they secretly induced men to say, "We have heard him speak blasphemous words against Moses and God." And they stirred up the people, the elders, and the scribes, and they came up to him and dragged him away, and brought him before the Council. They put forward false witnesses who said, "This man does not stop speaking against this holy place and the Law; for we have heard him say that this Nazarene, Jesus, will destroy this place and change the customs which Moses handed down to us." —Acts 6:8–14

The martyrdom of Stephen was triggered by false witnesses and false accusations. Stephen's opponents likely bribed the false witnesses to say the things they did, as indicated by the expression "secretly induced" (v. 11). The accusations contained a snippet of truth or a factoid. These data points, taken out of context and wrongly reported, created a false narrative. This resulted in a "stirring up" of the people (v. 12), who dragged Stephen away. The creation of false narratives borne by false witnesses is a common demonic tactic in bringing persecution upon Christians. It is no wonder that God commanded "Thou shalt not bear false witness" (Exodus 20:16, KJV). This demonic strategy resulted in the church receiving her first martyr.

These false accusations brought Stephen into the courtroom of the Sanhedrin. The result of the case was Stephen being dragged out and painfully stoned to death. However, there were many victories in Stephen's story.

First, God caused Stephen's face to shine like the face of an angel as he gave his testimony (Acts 6:15). This must have remained long imprinted upon the memories of those who saw it. Second, Stephen was able to preach a full sermon to the Sanhedrin. Through this powerful message, Stephen astutely interpreted the history of Israel and Messiah's place in that history. Stephen preached the true narrative, countering the false narratives and lies flying all around him. We can learn much from this today as we confront a tsunami of fake news and anti-Christian false narratives. Truly, Stephen delivered a breathtaking sermon. We will visit it again in chapter 3.

Third, Stephen asked forgiveness for those killing him. That prayer would be answered as young Saul of Tarsus, part of the attacking party, would later be converted to Christ on the road to Damascus. Fourth, as he was being martyred, Stephen saw the heavens open and the glory of God. He testified: "Behold, I see the heavens opened and the Son of Man standing at the right hand of God" (Acts 7:56). Possibly this was the glory illuminating his face and causing it to shine like the face of an angel.

Fifth, a "great persecution" arose against the Jerusalem church after the martyrdom of Stephen. In this manner, God used the martyrdom of Stephen to spur the church forward.

Now Saul approved of putting Stephen to death. And on
that day a great persecution began against the church in

Jerusalem, and they were all scattered throughout the regions of Judea and Samaria, except for the apostles.
—Acts 8:1

God used this great persecution to propel the church to its destiny to reach Judea, Samaria, and the ends of the earth. Acts 8:1 chronicles another stage in the fulfillment of Acts 1:8.

James, the Church's Second Martyr

Peter was arrested again in Acts 12. This time the secular leader Herod, seeking to please the Jews (12:3), threw Peter into prison. Herod executed James the brother of John (12:2). It appeared Peter would meet the same end in this earthly life but an angel rescued him from prison. Later in the same chapter, an angel would strike Herod dead.

Acts 12 gives us a chance to reflect. God striking Herod dead is not typical of the way he deals with tyrants. Many tyrants spend their days creating countless widows, orphans, and victims. Yet, few of them suffer for their sins in this lifetime. In fact, sometimes they pass on the evil rulership to their children or closest associates.

Not all Christians get rescued. Some, like James, get killed. Yet, Peter was rescued. Robert Gallagher notes in reference to this passage that sometimes it is difficult to understand why God rescues one believer and allows another one to die.[4] Yet, God used both instances to carry the church forward. The life-giving witness unto Christ by his bride continued unabated. Sometimes the intensity of the occasion surrounding persecution provides the greatest opportunity to witness. People's eyes and ears are opened unlike at other times.

Furthermore, the testimonies of martyrdom, such as Steven's, remained an important part of the church's devotional and spiritual life. This is reflected in early documents describing the martyrdoms of Polycarp of Smyrna and Perpetua of Carthage. Acts' focus on such narratives fortified and inspired believers well beyond the closing of the first century.

Expulsion

Though Christians typically endeavor to live peaceably with all people, sometimes unbelievers drive out Christians from the places where they live or have gone to minister. As described above, the "great persecution" of Acts 8:1 resulted in an expulsion of Christians from Jerusalem. This expulsion did not destroy the work of God but furthered it.

During the first missionary trip by Paul and Barnabas, a revival broke out in Pisidian Antioch. Paul and Barnabas, as was their missionary practice, began by preaching in the local synagogue. Acts 13 chronicles these amazing happenings. This revival triggered push-back in the heavenly places and a persecution in time and space:

> *The word of the Lord was being spread through the whole region. But the Jews incited the devout women of prominence and the leading men of the city, and instigated a persecution against Paul and Barnabas, and* drove them *out of their region. But they shook off the dust from their feet in protest against them and went to Iconium. And the disciples were continually filled with joy and with the Holy Spirit.* —Acts 13:49–52, emphasis added

This unholy alliance of persecutors drove Paul and Barnabas out of the city. While God's witnesses responded in protest by shaking the dust off their feet, they nonetheless rejoiced. Even during this persecution, Paul and Barnabas were filled with joy and the Holy Spirit.

Believers today still face expulsion. Even when being as discreet and sensitive as possible, the spirit of anti-Christ wages war against the body of Christ. For this reason, expulsion happens. While expulsion can interrupt believers' foreseeable life trajectory, we can nevertheless trust God that his plan will come to pass. Some flexibility is needed, as well as trust, discernment, and the need to look for God's "Plan B."

Legal Entanglements

Virtually all the events described thus far involved some type of legal entanglement. These legal entanglements can provide the opportunity for witness, as Jesus told us:

> *Now when they bring you before the synagogues and the officials and the authorities, do not worry about how or what you are to speak in your defense, or what you are to say; for the Holy Spirit will teach you in that very hour what you ought to say.* —Luke 12:11–12

Our goal must be to witness of the Lord Jesus Christ. This requires some spunk and defiance. Fear will suppress our witness. Jesus exhorted us to not worry. His conclusive word on the subject is: "do not be afraid of those who kill the body but are unable to kill the soul; but rather fear Him who is able to destroy both soul and body in hell" (Matthew 10:28).

Often the devil uses legal entanglements to emotionally wear down Christians. We will fully examine legal entanglements and public trials in chapter 9 of this book. Luke, writing by the

Holy Spirit, dedicates the final quarter of the Acts of the Apostles to Paul's legal challenges. The Holy Spirit knew that the church throughout the ages would need instruction as well as examples of how to navigate the swirling torrents of the courtroom.

APPLICATION FOR THE CHURCH TODAY

All the forms of persecution found in Acts exist today. These include mocking, threats, imprisonment, physical assaults, legal entanglements, and martyrdom. Today, we as believers in Christ may find ourselves on the defensive. We are mocked. Our beliefs and values are ridiculed. In Western contexts, Islamic contexts, and Communist contexts, many biblical values and doctrines have been scorned. Yet, some open-minded inquirers are observing. Let us take the mantle of Peter and pivot to sharing the gospel. Let us not allow the work of God to stop because of ridicule.

Let us take time to process what is going on in our times. Let us not bury it under a cloak of silence. Faith is the key that will enable us to overcome the soft persecution of mocking and derision.

As he did with the early church, the Holy Spirit is able to turn a dire situation into something special. Even martyrdom can be used to glorify God, showing he is worthy of our reciprocal devotion. Paul wrote about this reciprocal love: "For the love of Christ controls us, having concluded this, that one died for all, therefore all died; and he died for all, so that those who live would no longer live for themselves, but for Him who died and rose on their behalf" (2 Corinthians 5:14–15).

Episodes in history exist in which the church came under severe persecution, military conquest, or genocide. The North African church, once a thriving center of Christian life and theology, was largely eliminated westward of Egypt by the Arab Islamic invasion of the seventh century. Berber Christians fled to the mountains. Eventually, they were Islamized. Yet, in these days, the Holy Spirit has breathed life into them again as he reminds the Berbers of their Christian roots.

The church of the East, planted by Nestorian missionaries, was nearly exterminated during the Mongol invasion. That church was the largest Christian body, geographically, in its time. Their legacy continues. In places like Uzbekistan and China, new generations of believers in Christ are coming to discover that others have gone before them.

Political leadership sets the climate in which the church serves. Communist leaders in the former Soviet Union brazenly claimed they would stamp out the church. However, the church outlived those political leaders.

Christians were distributed relatively equally across the Korean Peninsula prior to the Communist takeover and partition of North Korea. Communist leaders have turned North Korea into a virtual concentration camp. Countless believers have met a martyr's death in the North. In free South Korea, fertile spiritual soil has resulted in the world's largest churches and most missionaries sent out per capita. Therefore, pastors should not state nonchalantly that neither political leadership nor form of government matters. Just ask Koreans.

More Application for the Church Today

What is the key for the church today as it encounters persecution? It is to be alert and to stand for Christ, no matter what. Paul writes to the Corinthians: "Be on the alert, *stand firm in the faith,* act like men, be strong" (1 Corinthians 16:13, emphasis added).

The enemy of our souls seeks to weaken and ultimately destroy our faith in Christ. He is not simply looking to cause pain and misery. Being alert to this, we must stand tenaciously in our faith in Christ.

Standing in faith is not a work of the flesh or simply an exercise of will-power. God is the one who enables us to stand. Even the weaker brother can stand when fortified by the Holy Spirit:

> *"Who are you to judge the servant of another? To his own master he stands or falls; and he will stand, for the Lord is able to make him stand."* —Romans 14:4

Now is the time to be alert and stand in Christ. When the early church experienced its first persecution through mocking, Acts notes that Peter not only spoke to the crowd but that he took a stand:

> *"But Peter,* taking his stand *with the other eleven, raised his voice and declared to them: 'Men of Judea and all you who live in Jerusalem, know this, and pay attention to my words.'"* —Acts 2:14, emphasis added

Yes, the Lord is able to make Christians stand firm! The gates of hell shall not prevail over the church of the Lord Jesus Christ.

FOR FURTHER DISCUSSION

Read Acts 4:18–31.

- Do we find ourselves under pressure not to speak or teach in the name of Jesus?

- If so, where is that pressure coming from and what is the purpose behind it?

- Which subjects are restricted or may trigger pushback or persecution?

- How can we best respond to it?

- How did the disciples respond to the threats made against them?

- How can we apply their response to our situations today?

CHAPTER 2

THE ACTS OF
THE HOLY SPIRIT

The first three chapters of this book describe themes that extend throughout Acts. The previous chapter addressed persecution—and how the Lord helped believers overcome it. This chapter considers how the Holy Spirit was working in the lives of the earliest believers in Christ. The Acts of the Apostles is the family history of all Christians. Acts is not the possession of any subset of one group of Christians. All believers in Christ need to learn what we can from this precious book of Scripture.

Father, Son, and Holy Spirit Usher in the Book of Acts

Prior to the book of Acts, the Holy Spirit's divine identity was hinted at but not well known. Jesus was physically present on this earth until his ascension in Acts 1:9. In the opening passage of Acts, Jesus speaks of Father, Son, and Spirit. Luke, the author, is guided by the Spirit as he gives this account:

The first account I composed, Theophilus, about all that Jesus began to do and teach, until the day when He was taken up to heaven, after He had given orders by the Holy Spirit to the apostles whom He had chosen. To these He also presented Himself alive after His suffering, by many convincing proofs, appearing to them over a period of forty days and speaking of things regarding the kingdom of God. Gathering them together, He commanded them not to leave Jerusalem, but to wait for what the Father had promised, "Which," He said, "you heard of from Me; for John baptized with water, but you will be baptized with the Holy Spirit not many days from now." So, when they had come together, they began asking Him, saying, "Lord, is it at this time that You are restoring the kingdom to Israel?" But He said to them, "It is not for you to know periods of time or appointed times which the Father has set by His own authority; but you will receive power when the Holy Spirit has come upon you; and you shall be My witnesses both in Jerusalem and in all Judea, and Samaria, and as far as the remotest part of the earth." —Acts 1:1–8

As the church was about to be launched into the world, we observe the Father, Son, and Holy Spirit working together—the Holy Trinity, Three in One. The Father was working. The Father promised the Holy Spirit (v. 4). The Father appointed times and seasons by his own authority (v. 7).

The Son was also working. Luke's gospel chronicles that which Jesus began to do and teach (v. 1). In Acts, Jesus will continue to do and to teach through his church. Jesus the Son presented himself alive to his disciples by many convincing proofs (v. 3). These resurrection appearances bolstered the faith of the disciples and prepared them for their coming ministry.

The Holy Spirit was also working. He is also featured in Luke's introduction. The orders given to Jesus' apostles are "by the Holy Spirit" (v. 2), reflecting complete unity between the Son and Spirit. Jesus promised his disciples that they would soon be baptized in the Holy Spirit (v. 5). The Spirit would provide the power (Greek, *dunamis*) for the apostles to witness throughout the world (v. 8). In this verse, missions by the church in the power of the Spirit was born.

An Overview of the Holy Spirit's Role in Acts

Acts 1:8 is quoted above. To refresh, Jesus tells his disciples: "you will receive power when the Holy Spirit has come upon you; and you shall be My witnesses both in Jerusalem and in all Judea, and Samaria, and as far as the remotest part of the earth." Throughout the book of Acts, the Holy Spirit empowered these disciples to be witnesses of Christ. The power of the Holy Spirit expanded the identity of Jesus' followers from disciples ("learners") to apostles ("sent ones").

In summary, the primary role of the Holy Spirit in Acts is to empower the apostles to witness of the Lord Jesus Christ. Thus, the Spirit seeks to glorify Christ. Jesus earlier told his disciples regarding the Holy Spirit: "*He will glorify Me*, for He will take from Mine and will disclose it to you" (John 16:14, emphasis added).

By the beginning of the Acts narrative, the Lord Jesus Christ was known in Galilee and Judea. The disciples on the Road to Emmaus were surprised when the Lord seemed not to know about the events regarding his crucifixion. However, this "Jesus movement" was still relatively small.

By the conclusion of Acts some 30 years later, the Lord Jesus Christ was being worshipped from Israel to Ethiopia to Rome.

Thomas had gone as far as India, and Paul's sights were set on Spain. The Holy Spirit indeed glorified Jesus by empowering the witness of Jesus' apostles.

This growing missionary movement has spread to all the world today. We are in the kingdom of God today because the Holy Spirit moved so powerfully in Acts. He still moves in our days.

The name "Holy Spirit" appears 41 times in Acts. The Holy Spirit is also referred to as "The Spirit" (Acts 8:29; 8:39; 10:19; 11:12; 11:28; 20:22; 21:4). A pastor friend speaks of and prays to the Holy Spirit by dropping *The*. He will say, "Holy Spirit showed us." Or: "Thank you, Holy Spirit." This terminology is helpful since *The* can be misinterpreted to be impersonal, whereas *Holy Spirit* is as personal and knowable as the Father and the Son.

Pentecost: Holy Spirit Introduces Himself to the World

More can be said of Pentecost than time will allow in this section. Pentecost is traditionally held to be the birthday of the church. Jewish tradition holds that the Ten Commandments were revealed on Pentecost. Pentecost was the occasion of the Jewish Feast of First Fruits, known as *Shavuot*. Pentecost comprised one of the three pilgrimage feasts for observant Jews in the Old Testament era. It was for this reason that Jewish pilgrims from all over the diaspora were in Jerusalem worshipping when the Acts 2 narrative began:

> *When the day of Pentecost had come, they were all together in one place. And suddenly a noise like a violent rushing wind came from heaven, and it filled the whole house where they were sitting. And tongues that looked like fire appeared to them, distributing themselves, and a tongue rested on each one of them. And they were all filled*

with the Holy Spirit and began to speak with different tongues, as the Spirit was giving them the ability to speak out. Now there were Jews residing in Jerusalem, devout men from every nation under heaven. —Acts 2:1–5

The Holy Spirit poured himself out on the Day of Pentecost in a way that would touch the nations. This outpouring would be observed and experienced by Jewish pilgrims from all over the Jewish world. They returned to the lands in which they lived with the experiences, giftings, and testimonies of Pentecost. As such, Pentecost proved to be not only a catalyst for the Jerusalem church but also for Messianic Jewish believers dispersed throughout the Jewish Diaspora.

Not Every Rushing Wind Is the Holy Spirit, but the Spirit Does Come like the Wind

It is beyond the scope of this book to consider all the types of Christian worship—Pentecostal or otherwise, liturgical or free-form. On Pentecost, the Holy Spirit came as a rushing wind. In the Indonesian revivals of the 1960s and 1970s, believers testified on occasion that the Spirit came like a rushing wind, and even that their church buildings appeared from the outside to be on fire.[5]

When believers are in a sleepy, near-sedated state, it is likely that the Spirit is neither moving nor being welcomed to move. However, neither volume nor crescendo of noise automatically indicates a move of the Spirit.

God wanted to encourage the isolated Old Testament prophet Elijah. Elijah was so discouraged that he prayed, "Enough! Now, LORD, take my life, for I am no better than my fathers" (1 Kings 19:4). He was a depressed and persecuted believer. In this time of need, God revealed himself to his prophet. Several powerful acts of nature occurred but God was not in them. He did not reveal himself in the rushing wind on this occasion but in the still small voice in the heart of the believer that was more like a gentle breath:

> *So [God] said, "Go out and stand on the mountain before the* Lord*." And behold, the* Lord *was passing by! And a great and powerful wind was tearing out the mountains and breaking the rocks in pieces before the* Lord*; but the* Lord *was not in the wind. And after the wind there was an earthquake, but the* Lord *was not in the earthquake. And after the earthquake, a fire, but the* Lord *was not in the fire; and after the fire, a sound of a gentle blowing. When Elijah heard it, he wrapped his face in his cloak and went out and stood in the entrance of the cave. And behold, a voice came to him and said, "What are you doing here, Elijah?"* —1 Kings 19:11–13

Flash and fanfare should not immediately be assumed to be a move of the Holy Spirit. Rather, when God's presence floods into the hearts of people, we can credit this to the moving of the Spirit of God. And when the fruit of the Spirit grows in the hearts of believers, we can be sure the Spirit is at work.

The Spirit came in like a rushing wind in Acts 2. There is also the move of the Spirit like a wind that changes the inner being of believers. Jesus explained this to Nicodemus: "The wind blows where it wishes, and you hear the sound of it, but you do not know where it is coming from and where it is going; so is everyone who has been born of the Spirit" (John 3:8).

Normally, we *see* the impact of the wind as it moves the clouds and bends the trees. If we sit inside and cannot see outside, we can *hear* the sound of the wind. Nicodemus came by night to speak with Jesus, so the wind on that night would have been heard and not seen. The Spirit moves like an internal wind in the lives of believers in Christ. Those who know them may have expected a certain trajectory, but then God turns their lives around. While on a mission to South America, I met another missionary from my hometown. It turns out that I went to high school with her first cousin, though I had not been a Christian at that time. She said she would immediately contact her and let her know we had met in South America. I replied, "I don't think she will believe that I am now a Christian missionary."

The Spirit also changes the direction of nations. South Korea sends thousands of missionaries into the world. Many Muslims expect that Christian missionaries would hail from places such as England and the USA. Some are amazed when they learn that vast numbers of South Koreans are Christians, and their churches are among the largest in the world. Africa, once known as the "Dark Continent," can now be considered the Continent of Light. Africa may be home to half the world's Christians within several decades, including many believers of strong faith.

The Role of the Spirit in the Lives of Unbelievers

Some may wonder about the relationship of the Holy Spirit to adherents of non-Christian religions. We observe godly and sincere people in other religions, as well as some virtuous people with no religious affiliation. Can these non-Christians have a relationship with God? What is the Holy Spirit's role in their lives?

Jesus explicitly stated about the Spirit that he can indeed work in the lives of unbelievers: "And He, when He comes, *will convict the world regarding sin,* and righteousness, and judgment: regarding sin, because they do not believe in Me" (John 16:8–9, emphasis added).

Therefore, unbelievers do not possess Christ or the Holy Spirit, but the Holy Spirit may graciously come to convict them of their sins. He can help them realize they need a Savior—the Lord Jesus Christ. The Holy Spirit may impress this need upon their unregenerate spirits in a process we call conviction. On the other hand, we must reject religious pluralism and its premise that God is genuinely present and working through non-biblical religions.

Examples of Holy Spirit Empowerment in Acts

In the Acts of the Apostles, the disciples of Jesus, who often stumbled and bumbled during their early training, were transformed into different men. Holy Spirit empowerment made the disciples of Jesus into different people. They became better disciples and more effective witnesses. Importantly, they became able to carry and extend the authority of the Lord Jesus Christ. Jesus must have looked down from heaven and rejoiced over what he observed.

Acts provides many examples of the Holy Spirit filling believers. Through what Luke specifically chronicles as the "filling of the Holy Spirit," the disciples:

- Spoke in other tongues as the Spirit gave utterance (2:4)
- Preached the gospel (4:8)
- Spoke the word of God with boldness (4:31)
- Beheld the glory of God (7:55)
- Received sight (9:17)
- Rebuked those opposing the work of God (13:9)

We can learn from how the Spirit filled these early believers, for the Spirit is still working in and through the church. The Acts narrative demonstrates that the filling of the Spirit manifested in many ways—always to glorify Jesus.

The Spirit's Guidance in Ministry

Believers must remain sensitive to the Spirit's leading when he sends foreigners into their lives. These "life intersections" may not be a coincidence. Hospitality, friendship, a word of witness, or an offer to pray in the name of Jesus may open the door to life in the Spirit for these new friends.

Christians serving internationally must likewise be sensitive to the Holy Spirit's leading. In Acts 16:6, during Paul's second missionary journey, Luke writes: "They passed through the Phrygian and Galatian region, after being forbidden by the Holy Spirit to speak the word in Asia." The Spirit empowered them *not to preach* in Asia Minor. God needed these particular apostles in Europe at this time. They would soon receive the Macedonian vision. Later, in God's timing, the Holy Spirit would lead these apostles and others back to Ephesus (Acts 18–19).

The lesson here is important for all believers. The Holy Spirit opens doors that no man can close. At other times, the Holy Spirit closes doors. Christians should maintain a prayerful and sensitive spiritual connection to God. Jesus is the Good Shepherd. He said his sheep will hear his voice. This principle is critical in ministry. Good decision making based on common sense and experiences is good but it was not sufficient for the apostles to fulfill their missionary ministry. They needed to be sensitive to the Spirit's leading.

The Holy Spirit's Leadership in Spiritual Warfare

Acts narrates the expansion of the kingdom of God. When the kingdom of God expands, spiritual opposition ensues. The Holy Spirit leads the charge in defeating unclean spirits. The battle is spirit against spirit. The Holy Spirit is the most powerful spirit in the universe.

Ephesus was a leading site of paganism and demonic activity. The Ephesians were in an unclean, binding covenant with their female goddess, Artemis. Her temple was located in the city and was known as one of the Seven Wonders of the World. Apostolic preaching would destroy the worship of Artemis. Later, Paul would write to the Ephesians:

> *Finally, be strong in the Lord and in the strength of His might. Put on the full armor of God, so that you will be able to stand firm against the schemes of the devil. For our struggle is not against flesh and blood, but against the rulers, against the powers, against the world forces of this darkness, against the spiritual forces of wickedness in the heavenly places.* —Ephesians 6:10–12

Throughout Acts, the Holy Spirit empowered the apostles to overcome evil spirits. They would never have been able to do so in their own power. Likewise, the Holy Spirit empowers believers today for ministry.

APPLICATION FOR THE CHURCH TODAY

The Comfort of the Holy Spirit causes the Church to Grow

For 2,000 years, the church has been growing and expanding. This growth cannot be credited to human activity, well-run committee meetings, or even strategic planning. According to

Acts, the comfort of the Holy Spirit caused the early church to grow. "So the church throughout Judea, Galilee, and Samaria enjoyed peace, as it was being built up; and as it continued in the fear of the Lord and in *the comfort of the Holy Spirit*, it kept increasing" (Acts 9:31, emphasis added).

To understand this dynamic, recall that Jesus told the disciples he would send the Holy Spirit, who was known as the Comforter, or Helper:

> *"I will ask the Father, and He will give you another Helper, so that He may be with you forever; the Helper is the Spirit of truth, whom the world cannot receive, because it does not see Him or know Him; but you know Him because He remains with you and will be in you."*
> —John 14:16–17

The church continues to grow even in high-persecution contexts through the comfort of the Holy Spirit. In Muslim lands, atheistic lands, or Communist lands, believers encounter much pain. Sometimes the obstacles rising against the church seem insurmountable. Yet, the Holy Spirit brings help, comfort, and grace. In my own life, I cannot fathom how I came into the kingdom of God or even remain in it. Thank you, Lord, for the grace of God and the comfort of the Holy Spirit!

FOR FURTHER DISCUSSION

Read Acts 1:6–8.

- What does it mean to be a "witness" for Jesus?

- Is this becoming easier or more difficult as time goes on?

- Which spiritual forces or ideologies oppose the witness for Christ?

- How is Holy Spirit empowering Christians today to be more effective witnesses for Christ?

CHAPTER 3

THE BIBLE STUDENTS

In the Muslim world, a group of Qur'anic students has made a name for itself in recent decades. They call themselves *Taliban*, meaning "Students," based on the Arabic word for "to ask." Students ask questions of their teachers. The Taliban are students of the Qur'an. As Christians, we can learn something from their commitment to their holy book, errant as the contents of that book might be.

For Christians, the Bible constitutes the primary spiritual fortification at times of persecution. According to Psalm 119:105, the word of God is "a lamp to my feet and a light to my path." The Bible will guide us through dark days. Christians grounded in the Bible will be best able to stand during the upcoming trials and tribulations.

Given these realities, those who oppose the gospel do everything in their power to limit the printing, distribution, public reading, and preaching of the Bible. In some Western countries, biblical standards of morality have been equated with hate speech. Soviet Communists notably forbade preaching from passages on the Second Coming of Christ, as this teaching contested their doctrine of the final triumph of communism.

Islam teaches that the Bible has been "corrupted" and superseded by the Qur'an.

All these competing worldviews see the Bible as a spiritual force that must be opposed. Some, such as Muslim scholars, are quick to misinterpret the Bible, finding Muhammad within its pages. When I was a new Christian back in the 1980s, our college group went on an outreach during which a "gay pastor" stepped forward from the crowd and rebuked us, saying, "Jesus said, 'Judge not, lest you be judged.'" Secularists throughout the Western world have long since banished the Bible from public schools, while no similar ban constricts basic teaching about the holy books of other faiths. All these realities and trends indicate Christians must take an uncompromising stand on the Bible.

The Importance of the Scriptures to the Apostles

Returning our focus to the Acts of the Apostles, it is evident that Jesus' disciples experienced a remarkable transformation. In the Gospels, they were concerned about what to eat. They inquired about who would gain power in Jesus' coming earthly kingdom. Satan was even able to sift Peter, a leader of the disciples, like wheat.

In Acts, however, the disciples of Jesus, aggregately, became more godly people. Their priorities shifted from earth to heaven. God transformed their character from that of cowardly mice to courageous lions. How did this happen? Their commitment to, and reliance upon, the Scriptures provided one key to this stunning transformation.

This was a work in progress. Jesus insisted to the disciples that somehow it would be to their advantage when he physically left them:

But now I am going to Him who sent Me; and none of you asks Me, "Where are You going?" But because I have said these things to you, grief has filled your heart. But I tell you the truth: it is to your advantage that I am leaving; for if I do not leave, the Helper will not come to you; but if I go, I will send Him to you. —John 16:5–7

Jesus, in leaving the disciples physically, did not leave them spiritually. From heaven, Jesus interceded for those women and men who walked with him during his earthly ministry. Hebrews teaches us about the Lord Jesus: "He is also able to save forever those who come to God through Him, since He always lives to make intercession for them" (Hebrews 7:25).

So, the early church was strengthened by the coming of the Spirit and the intercession of Jesus. Additionally, the Holy Spirit would cause the disciples to remember Jesus' words to them: "These things I have spoken to you while remaining with you. But the Helper, the Holy Spirit whom the Father will send in My name, He will teach you all things, and *remind you of all that I said to you*" (John 14:25–26, emphasis added). Through these reminders, the Holy Spirit would inspire the four Gospels about to be written and the apostolic preaching that was about to change the world.

Burning Hearts and the Full Breadth of Scripture

Jesus spent three wonderful years with his twelve disciples. He spent focused time with the inner circle of Peter, James, and John. Around them was a wider group of men and women whom Jesus taught and among whom he fellowshipped. Jesus instructed them by his life example and by opening the Old Testament Scriptures to them.

One glimpse of the type of teaching Jesus instilled was demonstrated when he taught two disciples on the Road to Emmaus. They were despondent that Jesus had been crucified. They failed to recognize their resurrected Savior. Their faith seemed to waver. Luke records, "Then beginning with Moses and with all the Prophets, He explained to them the things written about Himself in all the Scriptures" (Luke 24:27). Later, these disciples testified, "Were our hearts not burning within us when He was speaking to us on the road, while He was explaining the Scriptures to us?" (Luke 24:32).

The hearts of these disciples were set on fire as Jesus preached the full breadth of Scripture. They now had understanding. The missing puzzle pieces were found and put into place. Their faith was strengthened, and they were ready to witness.

Today, as we live in days of persecution, uncertainty, and wavering faith, we can learn much from how Jesus ministered to his disciples. After all, we are his disciples still. Jesus is still teaching men, women, and children Scripture. Theological degrees may be helpful but they are not indispensable for those who want to be used by God. The overcoming church will overcome its challenges through the fortification of the Bible.

Apostolic Preaching in Acts:
What Can We Learn from It?

In Acts, Luke records sermons from Peter, Stephen, and Paul. Their command of Scripture, which they quote from memory repeatedly, is stunning. In most cases, they did not have a week to prepare a message. In some cases, they were dragged, involuntarily, into places where they would immediately begin to witness of Christ. They demonstrate a breathtaking knowledge of the Old Testament. Not only do they quote Scripture but they appropriately place those Scriptures within biblical narratives that bring life and salvation to their listeners.

It becomes clear from reading Acts that the disciples of Jesus were not spending a lot of time on the news, politics, and sports. Self-confession here. Instead, these disciples of Jesus were poring over the Old Testament Scriptures. They no doubt gave significant time to Scripture memorization. It is impossible otherwise to explain the riveting Scripture-filled sermons that would follow. They had neither tablets nor teleprompters to assist them.

The disciples must have also strained their collective memories, helping each other to remember everything Jesus told them. And the Holy Spirit helped them to remember the things Jesus said. Matthew and John would later write their respective Gospels. Christian tradition holds that Peter dispensed much of what Jesus taught to Mark for the preparation of the second Gospel.

Muslims call Christians and Jews "People of the Book." That description certainly fit the early church. They became as comfortable in the Bible as squirrels or monkeys are in trees. Even though there were other experts in the Bible in those days—the Scribes—it was actually the disciples of Jesus who ably handled the Word of God. These disciples were able to do so because they were *willing to obey* the Scriptures, and because the Holy Spirit was helping them.

Peter's Sermons

Jesus spoke Simon Peter's identity into existence. He would be a rock. That identity would become a reality early in Acts. In Acts 1, Peter interpreted Judas' betrayal as fulfillment of Old Testament prophesies. He quoted Psalm 69:25 and Psalm 109:8. This interpretation helped the early church at a time of betrayal and uncertainty. Judas was quickly replaced by Matthias. Pentecost was just around the corner.

The previous chapter addressed the events of Pentecost. This section focuses on Peter's revelatory interpretation of those supernatural events. In what is known as "Peter's First Sermon" (Acts 2:14-36), he quoted from three Old Testament passages: Joel 2:28–32; Psalm 16:8–10; and Psalm 110:1. He alluded to at least two more verses: 2 Samuel 7:12; and Psalm 89:4.

Not only did Peter quote the Old Testament but he applied the passages to help people understand what was going on in that moment. His applications were prophetic in their impact. Peter built upon two great themes: Joel's promised Spirit outpouring, and David's prophecy from Psalm 16 about the Messiah's resurrection. The Spirit confirmed this powerful sermon by convicting the listeners. Hence, the revival of Pentecost began.

Soon thereafter, God miraculously healed the lame man at the Beautiful Gate. This miracle provided an occasion for Peter's "Second Sermon" (Acts 3:12-26). He did not re-use last week's sermon. Peter quoted from Deuteronomy 18, interpreting Jesus as that prophet like unto Moses. He then interpreted the Abrahamic blessing of Genesis 12 and 18 as being fulfilled in Christ. He wove quotes and interpretations together beautifully, again with profound effect.

This was the same Peter who a short time previously could not get out of his own way. He denied the Lord in his lonely hour.

Peter wept bitterly afterward. We should all be encouraged that the Holy Spirit can pick us up again no matter how many times we fall. Let us continue studying, memorizing, and meditating on the Bible, both personally and in our church groups. In doing so, we will be equipped to witness for Christ as Peter did, solid as a rock.

Stephen's Farewell Sermon

Stephen's defense in Acts 7 stands as a jewel of preaching in the 2,000-year history of the church. This servant of God was given a position as deacon so the leading apostles would not need to neglect the Word of God to wait on tables. Stephen proved himself able to wait on tables without neglecting the word of God. He was a mighty preacher:

> *Stephen, full of grace and power, was performing great wonders and signs among the people. But some men from what was called the Synagogue of the Freedmen, including both Cyrenians and Alexandrians, and some from Cilicia and Asia, rose up and argued with Stephen. But they were unable to cope with his wisdom and the Spirit by whom he was speaking.* —Acts 6:8–10

The high priest and Sanhedrin thought they had cornered Stephen but they were in for a surprise. As noted in chapter 1, they had bribed false witnesses to make false accusations against Stephen. The high priest most likely thought they had this uneducated dishwasher completely trapped. Even though he may have received reports that Stephen was a mighty preacher, he could not have believed his ears when he interrogated the deacon regarding the accusations: "Are these things so?" (Acts 7:1).

Stephen's audience was blessed to hear what may have been the greatest historical sermon ever preached. Luke's 50-verse narration records Stephen making at least 50 Old Testament quotes or references, according to the *Blue Letter Bible*.[6] Stephen quoted heavily from Genesis and Exodus to provide the whole redemptive history of Israel. He spoke of Abraham and Moses as people speak of their best friends.

Since the accusations pertained specifically to Moses, Stephen skillfully described Jesus as the prophet "like unto Moses" about whom Moses prophesied. He turned the tables on the Sanhedrin, the defendant becoming the plaintiff. He accused them of murdering the promised Messiah. This was as far as Stephen got before the crowd rushed forward and dragged him off to stone him. It seems unlikely that this could have happened without the high priest giving signals to either approve or command this execution.

Two comments preface Stephen's sermon of defense. First, New Testament sermons were likely sermon highlights. Every recorded spoken word is true. The Holy Spirit himself oversaw and inspired the writing of the New Testament books that include these sermons, including those of Jesus. I just read Stephen's sermon aloud as I sat at my desk. It took about seven minutes in a normal speaking voice, even though it is the longest sermon in Acts, and fills the longest chapter in Acts. A seven-minute court trial would be very brief in any era. Perhaps Luke did not record all the "fluff" of circumstances around the event, if indeed Stephen spoke longer than seven minutes. Yet, what the Holy Spirit wanted us to retain was recorded. What a sermon it was.

Second, Stephen had no opportunity to prepare this message. He was essentially ambushed and hauled before the court. Sometimes we know we will give a sermon, a seminar, a lecture, or a class on such-and-such a date. We have time to prepare and practice. I prefer not to speak with many notes but I usually prepare an outline. I review it and hopefully know it essentially by heart before I speak. Stephen had no such opportunity for preparation.

The depth and breadth of Stephen's sermon indicate that the early believers spent a sizable portion of their time together in Bible study. They pored over the Old Testament and rehearsed what Jesus had told them. They internalized the Bible so that they could externalize it in witness for Christ.

Paul's Sermons

The apostle Paul typically began his missionary outreaches by preaching in a synagogue if one could be found. Afterward, he would expand the focus of his ministry to the Gentiles in that community. Paul's sermons to Jewish audiences were quite different than the ones he preached to Gentile audiences. In what we understand as "contextualization," Paul's Mars Hill sermon does not include Old Testament references. His audience had no idea what the Old Testament was. Yahweh was unknown to them. Their Stoic scholars lived in spiritual ignorance.

Like Peter and Stephen, Paul relied heavily on the Hebrew Scriptures when preaching to Jewish audiences. Luke presents several excellent examples of these sermons during Paul's first missionary journey. Chapter 1 recounted the persecution that arose in Pisidian Antioch. Prior to that persecution, Paul preached in the synagogue there. The synagogue officials invited Paul to address the people:

"After the reading of the Law and the Prophets, the synagogue officials sent word to them, saying, 'Brothers, if you have any word of exhortation for the people, say it'" (Acts 13:15). It is likely some of his brethren later would have rebuked him for such an invitation, the situation turning out as it did. But Paul was ready.

Paul's sermon at the synagogue of Pisidian Antioch was a pearl of preaching. According to the *Blue Letter Bible*,[7] this sermon included 20 Old Testament references, including several direct quotations. In an example of Old Testament bridging, Paul took the angle of Christ being the Son of David:

> *After He [God] had removed him [Saul], He raised up David to be their king, concerning whom He also testified and said, "I have found David, the son of Jesse, a man after My heart, who will do all My will." From the descendants of this man, according to promise, God has brought to Israel a Savior, Jesus.* —Acts 13:22–23

Paul's message in Pisidian Antioch catalyzed the Galatian revivals in that part of Asia Minor. Both Jews and Gentiles came into Christ's kingdom because of this preaching and the accompanying signs and wonders.

To summarize, early church leaders such as Peter, Stephen, and Paul animated the spiritual forefathers, including Abraham, Joseph, Moses, David, and Solomon. They interpreted their lives and ministries as pointing to Christ. They demonstrated an amazing grasp of the Bible. The study of Scripture must have been the top priority of their lives.

While we can surmise that Paul's training as a Pharisee provided him much biblical data prior to his encounter with

Jesus, the same would not have been true of Jesus' other apostles. Jesus' chosen twelve included fishermen and a tax collector. Peter kept kosher and testified that nothing unclean had ever entered his mouth. However, his grasp of the Old Testament was likely limited before he met Jesus.

The New Testament writings of Matthew, Mark, Luke, John, Paul, James, Peter, and Jude testify that they were astute students of the Old Testament. They form part of a wider movement of the early church in which Bible study and application played a preeminent and an inestimable role. In short, the early church was a church of Bible students.

APPLICATION FOR THE CHURCH TODAY

I recall being part of a church renowned for its excellent Christmas and Easter dramatic plays. My wife, our youngest son, and I decided to audition for the Easter play. Apparently, I did not do well during the audition, because I was given the role of Lazarus—perhaps the most important biblical figure who never speaks! I only needed to die, stink, and revive. I needed to wait out in the hallway until Jesus called out, "Lazarus, come forth!" The play director solemnly warned me that I must not miss this cue, or I would single-handedly humiliate Jesus and ruin the performance!

Unfortunately, I was absent for the first practice, at which scripts were distributed. At several subsequent practices, the director did not bring a copy of the script for me. This caused me some anxiety as I could not follow where we were in the presentation—increasing the chance I might miss the important call, "Lazarus, come forth!"

Whenever a break in practice occurred, I would ask another person on the cast to borrow their script, poring over it as fast and voraciously as I could. Everything depended on this script. I was desperate to devour it. About that time, I became convicted that my hunger to see that script dwarfed my hunger to devour the Holy Bible. The Scriptures are indeed the "script of life."

In times of persecution, the Bible fortifies the church. In extreme cases, oppressors deny Christians access to Scripture. At these times, previous study and memorization are key in helping the believers stand. I have heard of American prisoners during the Vietnam War culling their collective memories to recall the Bible verses they had memorized as children. Such verses can strengthen believers. Sometimes persecution of this magnitude can spur the backslidden to return to faith in the Lord.

Stephen was the church's first martyr. Stephen's example provides persecuted believers a golden standard. He applied the individual verses and passages he quoted as a part of the overall biblical narrative. No doubt there was an element to the Holy Spirit helping him know what to say. But previous Bible study and memorization must have played an important part in Stephen's glorious day.

Today, hunger for the Bible pales in comparison to the early believers who ran the race before us. The word of God will help us to stand in times of persecution. In Paul's description of the armor of God, he notes that the sword of the Spirit is the Word of God: "And take the helmet of salvation and the sword of the Spirit, which is the word of God" (Ephesians 6:17). The Bible will equip us for witness, as many souls will become open to the gospel during times of adversity.

FOR FURTHER DISCUSSION

Read Acts 3:17–21 from Peter's Second Sermon.

- How does Peter's reliance on messages "from the mouths of the prophets" (see verses 18 and 21) demonstrate his reliance on the Old Testament?

- Describe a situation in which the Bible brought you "times of refreshing" (verse 19).

- In what ways is the message of the Bible or biblical teachings under attack today?

- How can the Bible fortify us for the days ahead?

CHAPTER 4

SOLOMON'S PORTICO

The physical gathering together of believers in Christ is sacred. Jesus said that he would be in their midst. Like our brothers and sisters in past generations, believers in Christ today in many places face increasing governmental restrictions and even church closures. The questions multiply: "Where to meet?" "How to meet?" "Do we need to meet at all?" "Is meeting online adequate to meet the needs of believers?"

Comfort Zones and Revival Zones

One often hears Christians say, "God moves in mysterious ways." This precept applies to Christian missions, too. God's plan for revival among the nations frequently requires Christians to move out of our "comfort zones" to attempt great things for the King of Kings.

In this chapter, I will describe how Jesus' apostles moved out of their comfort zone in Galilee to start the New Testament church in Judea. Even in this high-persecution context, the disciples did not forsake meeting together. Rather, they kept meeting together as a priority. I will include a few applications to the difficult and unprecedented times we face in the coronavirus era and beyond. Finally, I will examine how Christians and churches must move out of our comfort zones to keep meeting together and witnessing for Christ.

What is a "Comfort Zone?"

We have been told to beware of eating too much "comfort food," such as ice cream! For frequent airline travelers, there is a question of what exactly qualifies as an "emotional support animal" that brings comfort to its traveling owner? Not long ago, someone brought a small horse on an airplane as an emotional support animal.[8] It is unclear how comfortable this scenario was for others in that aisle!

When we speak of "comfort zones," we usually refer to areas or contexts in which a person is likely to encounter a familiar, predictable, and pleasant experience. Sometimes this is applied to the thermostat: not too hot, not too cold, but just right.

Jesus' Disciples Move Out of Their Galilean Comfort Zone

Though Jesus was born in Bethlehem of Judea, he temporarily found refuge with his mother Mary and Joseph in Egypt. Yet, he grew up in Nazareth of Galilee. Jesus launched his public ministry in Galilee, frequenting the fishing villages around the Sea of Galilee. From there, he called his twelve disciples. All of them were Galileans.

Jesus of course knew that their story would not end in Galilee. His crucifixion was destined to take place in Jerusalem of Judea. Over Jesus' three years of public ministry, he and his disciples made a number of trips to Judea for ministry and to celebrate the appointed Jewish feasts.

Jerusalem was also the stronghold of the Jewish religious leadership. The Sanhedrin assembled in Jerusalem. This was the ruling body that (other than Nicodemus and Joseph of Arimathea) rejected Jesus as Messiah. Many of these leaders disrespected Galileans, claiming that no prophet could come out of Galilee. When Nicodemus tried to defend Jesus, his colleagues sneered at him: "You are not from Galilee as well, are you? Examine the Scriptures, and see that no prophet arises out of Galilee" (John 7:52).

Jesus' disciples became increasingly agitated and uncomfortable when visiting Judea (also known as "Judah"). Lazarus lived in Bethany near Jerusalem. When Jesus heard that Lazarus was sick, he waited two days. "Then after this He said to the disciples, 'Let's go to Judea again.' The disciples said to Him, 'Rabbi, the Jews were just now seeking to stone You, and yet You are going there again?'" (John 11:7–8).

It took a lot of convincing for Jesus to get the disciples to move out of their Galilean comfort zone. Thomas was full of faith that something bad would happen there: "Thomas, who was called Didymus, said to his fellow disciples, 'Let's also go, so that we may die with Him'" (John 11:16). For the disciples of Christ, Jerusalem and Judea were their "discomfort zone." Jesus' arrest, trials, and crucifixion would happen in Judea.

Peter "snapped" spiritually at the campfire but this was not the biggest error he made in that period of his life. After Jesus' resurrection, Peter was confused and disillusioned. He decided to return to the comfort zone of his former life as a fisherman on the Sea of Galilee:

Simon Peter, Thomas who was called Didymus, and Nathanael of Cana in Galilee, the sons of Zebedee, and two others of His disciples were together. Simon Peter said to them, "I am going fishing." They said to him, "We are also coming with you." They went out and got into the boat; and that night they caught nothing. —John 21:2–3

Not only did Peter leave the place where he could have had a fruitful ministry but he took over half of Jesus' disciples with him.

Jesus visited those disillusioned disciples. The divine carpenter once again showed the fishermen where to catch the fish. After the fish breakfast, Jesus asked Peter, "Simon, son of John, do you love Me more than these?" (John 21:15). The question seems to probe whether Peter loved the fish that represented his comfort zone more than the sheep he would soon shepherd as leader of the early church.

Before his ascension, Jesus re-assembled the full group of disciples and other followers in Jerusalem. He strictly warned them to stay in Jerusalem, not to return to their comfort zone of Galilee:

Gathering them together, He commanded them not to leave Jerusalem, but to wait for what the Father had promised, "Which," He said, "you heard of from Me; for John baptized with water, but you will be baptized with the Holy Spirit not many days from now." —Acts 1:4–5

When Jesus ascended, the angels spoke to the Galilean throng that thought they had been left as spiritual orphans in Judea:

"Men of Galilee, why do you stand looking into the sky?
This Jesus, who has been taken up from you into heaven,
will come in the same way as you have watched Him go
into heaven." —Acts 1:11

Creating a "Comforter Zone" of the Holy Spirit in Jerusalem

Praise God that the disciples obeyed Jesus by remaining in Judea. Soon a revival broke out, accompanied by signs and wonders. The Feast of Pentecost followed only ten days after Jesus' ascension. As noted in chapter 2, Acts 2 describes how the Jewish pilgrims had come to Jerusalem from all over the world for this feast. When the Holy Spirit, known as the Comforter, fell upon them as tongues of fire, the disciples began speaking in the various languages of the nations from which these pilgrims had come. "They were amazed and astonished, saying, 'Why, are not all these who are speaking Galileans?'" (Acts 2:7).

Peter, filled with the Holy Spirit, was able to interpret the Pentecost event and preach to the great crowd. Three thousand were saved that day and the church was born.

A First Meeting Place for the Early Church: Solomon's Portico

This growing group of followers of Jesus remained outside their comfort zone. They had no meeting place. This was hostile territory in which Jesus had just been arrested and executed. But they realized they could not escape to their Galilean comfort zone. They remembered seeing Jesus walking on the temple grounds: "At that time the Feast of the Dedication took place in Jerusalem; it was winter, and Jesus was walking in the temple area, in the portico of Solomon" (John 10:22–23). Solomon's Portico (also known as "Solomon's Porch" or "Solomon's Colonnade") was located within the temple walls but outside the temple building in which was located the Holy of Holies.

Miracles Happening

In Acts 3, Peter and John healed the lame man who sat begging at the Beautiful Gate. "While he was clinging to Peter and John, all the people ran together to them at the portico named Solomon's, completely astonished." (Acts 3:11). Solomon's Portico was the place the early church chose to meet. It was a place where they had seen Jesus walk, and where the Holy Spirit was now moving.

This first site of early church meetings also became known as a place of miracles: "At the hands of the apostles many signs and wonders were taking place among the people; and they were all together in Solomon's portico" (Acts 5:12). The Solomon's Portico site itself was not magical, nor was the name of the place of great importance. The key factor was God's united people meeting together to worship Jesus and testify of him. Solomon's Portico was a high-persecution area. The apostles would get arrested several times but at least the church had a place to meet. From this starting place in Jerusalem, they would spread the gospel throughout Judea, Samaria, and to the uttermost parts of the world.

Coronavirus, Distancing, and Comfort Zones

Fast forward to our days. The coronavirus has created challenges for holding corporate gatherings. Reaction to the virus has impacted houses of worship, including churches. Initially, churches in many countries were forbidden to meet in large groups. In many places, churches could only gradually begin to re-assemble with limited attendance and social distancing. In some cases, politicians seemed to promote a double-standard in which large political protests were allowed but large church gatherings were forbidden.

Large numbers of Christians have found themselves outside their spiritual comfort zones in this recent past. Having a familiar place of worship and routine is certainly a good thing. However, this has been upended in 2020 and beyond. Truly our pastors need much prayer as they navigate these types of situations. It is vital that believers regularly meet with other believers for worship. While being peaceable and compromising may serve well in some time periods, seasons of persecution require church leaders to stand firm.

Many churches and groups of worshippers have exercised creativity in holding church services. Feeding the flock has also required adding an online option but this cannot replace believers meeting together physically. Many believers have found the benefit of meeting in small groups. Churches may include a small-group format, which serves well in times of persecution. Spiritual isolation is a tool of Satan to bring discouragement. Today, believers need spiritual encouragement, as well as the courage to connect with other believers and unsaved inquirers.

Ministry in High-Persecution Contexts: Always a Trip Outside One's Comfort Zone!

Though persecution is a global phenomenon, I will provide a brief focus on Muslim contexts, which have long been considered hostile to the gospel. Christian ministry to Muslims has been going on for many centuries. Yet, ministry to Muslims often involves persecution, which almost always happens in a discomfort zone. The "Apostle to Islam" Samuel Zwemer went to the Persian Gulf area over a century ago. It was so hot and humid there that he used to do his writing with a wet towel wrapped around his head! He was out of his comfort zone. Yet Zwemer did not leave, even after burying his two young daughters in Bahrain in 1904 after they had died of dysentery.

Christians of Muslim Background (CMBs): A New Spiritual Home in the Church of Christ

Muslims who have come to faith in Christ face many challenges. Of course, there is the possibility of governmental persecution in many Muslim countries. In nearly all Muslim contexts, the convert, or CMB, will face family pressure. In some cases, nothing can be done to keep relationships with family and friends from rupturing.

A Turkish CMB named Ziya Meral wrote a booklet titled *No Place to Call Home.*[9] The title itself sums up the challenges facing CMBs. Many are disowned or shunned by family, friends, and community. In some cases, Christians are wary of Muslims who claim to have become Christians. Wherever trust remains weak, no positive comfort zone can develop.

In our days, as more Muslims are coming to Christ, we are witnessing positive developments. First, the thought of a Muslim coming to Christ is no longer unheard of among Muslims. Therefore, the stigma of conversion is decreasing, even though persecution may still be severe. Second, Christian churches are having more experiences welcoming CMBs into their midst. This experience is no longer so far outside their comfort zone. Third, in some contexts, new churches made up of CMBs have sprung up. These mother churches are birthing daughter churches. The church is dear to CMBs. Finally, internet resources for CMBs are multiplying, which can help offset social or spiritual isolation.

The Uttermost Parts of the Earth Includes Muslim Contexts

This is God's day of harvest for Muslims. The Holy Spirit is drawing Muslims out of allegiance to Muhammad and the Qur'an and into the Lord Jesus Christ. This means leaving the religious comfort zone of Islam and the familiar ways of praying toward Mecca. Ultimately, CMBs are finding the place of comfort in the Comforter, who is the Holy Spirit!

We all have a part to play in this end-time revival. In some cases, it will require us leaving our own comfort zones to put ourselves into a place of proximity to Muslims who are interested in the gospel. In doing so, our discomfort may be swallowed up in the comfort of the presence of God. As Paul stated:

> *Blessed be the God and Father of our Lord Jesus Christ, the Father of mercies and God of all comfort, who comforts us in all our affliction so that we will be able to comfort those who are in any affliction with the comfort with which we ourselves are comforted by God.*
> —2 Corinthians 1:3–4

As we have seen, in God's presence is fullness of joy. But a discomfort zone can emerge due to fear of the unknown and the unfamiliar. As agents of revival, our flexibility and trust in the Lord are needed greatly in this day of harvest! This is a day of action and intercession in seeing a great ingathering of unbelievers—even Muslims—into the kingdom of God.

APPLICATION FOR THE CHURCH TODAY

The meeting together of believers in Christ is sacred and cannot be abandoned. The early church met at Solomon's Portico in Jerusalem even though this location constituted a high-persecution area. They did not hide their ministry under a basket. Through the guidance of the Holy Spirit, they made wise and bold decisions, and the church continued to grow.

A pastor who served in the former Soviet Union stated that every home church meeting was a high-risk event. Any service could be raided by the police, resulting in believers receiving fines or even being dragged off in handcuffs. Sometimes pastors were sent to Siberia, with a possibility of never seeing their families again. This pastor stated that believers knew the risk but *the spiritual cost of not meeting was higher than the physical risk of meeting.* We can learn much from this wisdom.

Today, a strange virus has kept believers from one another. While a serious virus, it might be being used as a "trojan horse" by some who seek to exert greater societal control. We have been told by government leaders in many countries that church is not an "essential service." This is not true. Church is essential. Pastors will need to be both creative and courageous in making sure the flock can gather, even if this means upsetting long-established formats. Let us abide in faith at our Solomon's Porticoes, for there the Lord Jesus will be in the midst.

FOR FURTHER DISCUSSION

Read Acts 5:12.

- What lessons can be learned from the early church meeting together at Solomon's Portico?

- In what ways have gatherings of believers come under attack in our days?

- How might we need to be flexible in the coming days to keep meeting with other Christians?

CHAPTER 5

HONESTLY!

We live in a season of history marked by rampant dishonesty and fake news. This is not new in human history; Satan, the father of lies, lied to Eve in the Garden of Eden. That same lying spirit animates much of today's media. Social media giants and internet corporations now routinely use filtering techniques to suppress true information and to propagate false narratives.

Great care needs to be taken when consuming media. A spirit of anti-Christ pervades the times. Good is called evil and evil is called good. It is hard to know what to believe. What we hear and read needs to be filtered through the lens of Scripture. And it is more important than ever to recognize the voice of our Good Shepherd as myriad other voices clamor for attention and seek to lead believers astray. When Jesus' disciples asked him what will be the sign of the end of the age, indeed his first instruction was, "See to it that no one misleads you." (Matthew 24:4) So we can expect deception and misinformation to increase as the end draws near.

For these reasons, God made sure the early church was founded upon a standard of honesty. These principles provide invaluable guidance as the church today navigates troubled waters. The Holy Spirit provided a stark example in those early days in the case of Ananias and Sapphira.

The Holy Spirit Puts His Foot Down: The Story of Ananias and Sapphira

The Acts of the Apostles narrates the spiritual gifts in operation as churches were planted. Miracles occur on nearly every page. Another important but often overlooked question today is that of *character qualities*. Which character quality is most important for new churches and new believers? Upon which area did God himself place emphasis in the book of Acts?

Honestly, it's honesty.

With a vision toward strong biblical discipleship and church planting, greater attention must be devoted to one specific biblical virtue: *honesty*. Honesty creates an environment in which leaders can work together. Without honesty, it is impossible to enjoy trust. Without trust, it is impossible to experience healthy relationships. Without healthy relationships, church plants will crumble. We may humbly confess that Christ's church, 2,000 years after its inception, is not the epitome of honesty that we so desire.

Acts is largely an encouraging chronicle of the birth and growth of the early church. Of course, that growth took place in many contexts where persecution was also happening. A major internal scandal rocked the church in Acts 5. Many of the early believers had sacrificially sold lands and houses to support those in the growing movement who were in need (Acts 4:34).

In the case of Ananias and Sapphira, they were under no explicit command to sell their property. Ananias did so voluntarily.

But he hatched a dishonest plan with his wife to make that sale, keeping back a portion from what he would donate to the church. It is likely the amount he gave the apostles was at least credible. Nevertheless, he wanted to get credit for a full sale, while secretly keeping back some for himself. Ananias formed a conspiracy of dishonesty with his wife in the hope of deceiving the apostles.

In condemning this dishonesty, God ended their lives. Possibly they were so internally distressed by their dishonesty that they each had a heart attack when called out by Peter. The physiological diagnosis at this point is not so important. Peter told Ananias that he had lied to God:

> *Ananias, why has Satan filled your heart to lie to the Holy Spirit and to keep back some of the proceeds of the land? While it remained unsold, did it not remain your own? And after it was sold, was it not under your control? Why is it that you have conceived this deed in your heart? You have not lied to men, but to God.* —Acts 5:3–4

At first glance, God's sentence may appear harsh. After all, Ananias and Sapphira gave a sizable offering to the church. Many Christians fall short in faithfully giving tithes and offerings. Few of us could say we have attained a one hundred percent lifetime record of faithfulness in this area. Yet, God does not strike us dead. Why, then, the severe judgment of Ananias and Sapphira?

Acts 5 indicates that God judged Ananias and Sapphira for dishonesty, not stinginess. It seems clear the Holy Spirit had put his foot down. God would not allow dishonesty to mark the early church in its formative period.

Paul's Insistence on an Honest and Straightforward Gospel Presentation

Paul ministered in diverse contexts, as shall be seen in subsequent chapters. Acts describes those missionary trips. Paul's epistles address follow-up concerns with the new believers and new churches. The first missionary trip by Paul and Barnabas from Antioch went first to Cyprus and then to the Galatian area of Asia Minor. In his subsequent Epistle to the Galatians, Paul addresses a controversy that reflects his emphasis on honesty and straightforwardness. That controversy involves the important issue of fellowship among believers:

> *But when Cephas came to Antioch, I opposed him to his face, because he stood condemned. For prior to the coming of some men from James, he used to eat with the Gentiles; but when they came, he began to withdraw and separate himself, fearing those from the circumcision. The rest of the Jews joined him in hypocrisy, with the result that even Barnabas was carried away by their hypocrisy. But when I saw that they were* not straightforward about the truth of the gospel, *I said to Cephas in the presence of all, "If you, being a Jew, live like the Gentiles and not like the Jews, how is it that you compel the Gentiles to live like Jews?* —Galatians 2:11–14, emphasis added

In this context, Paul saw that Peter was not being straightforward about the truth of the gospel (v. 14). This occurred, ironically, after Peter had experienced the great visions of unclean foods before the Gentile Pentecost at Cornelius' home described in Acts 10.

Later, during Paul's trial before Festus and Agrippa, the apostle states that none of their ministry had been done in secret (Acts 26:26). The Holy Spirit intended the apostles to be honest about their doctrines. None of their methods were secretive. They had observed Jesus himself teaching openly in the temple.

These teachings provide lessons for ministry today. While it may not be necessary to share everything with everyone, we should not say untrue things or be less than straightforward. Let unbelievers know for sure that Christians are honest people.

A Comparison: The Islamic View of Truth and Honesty

Coming from a Muslim background and having interacted with Muslims around the globe, one analysis is scarcely debatable: Muhammad's example regarding dishonesty has left deep scars upon the souls of Muslims. Many Muslims are now entering the kingdom of God, so repentance and correction are required. The deity presented by Muhammad is known as *al-Makar*, the schemer/deceiver god. Muhammad endorsed the use of deception and dissimulation (*taqiyya*) to further Islam. And the following hadith describes Muhammad's dishonesty and duplicity:

> *Narrated Um Kulthum bint Uqba: "That she heard Allah's Apostle saying, 'He who makes peace between the people by inventing good information or saying good things, is not a liar.'"* —Sahih Bukhari, Volume 3, Book 49, Number 857

This dishonesty dynamic now interfaces with the new missiological emphasis on the "Honor-Shame" worldview. In societies that *value honor over truth*, people routinely stretch the truth or outright lie to preserve honor. When "saving face" results in dishonesty, Christ is not glorified.

Given all these factors, I re-ask the question: which biblical emphasis is most important for Christians of a Muslim background (CMBs)? The same as for all Christians: honestly, it's honesty.

A Theology of Honesty

While Christians use the word "truth" frequently, we rarely hear mention of the associated biblical concept of "honesty." This section springboards from Acts 5 to lay out the biblical theology of honesty in effect during the early church. As such, we will examine biblical examples, and consider biblical terms such as "honest," "truth," and "confession." We will conclude with some applications for the church today.

What Happened?

We live in the universe God created. Time marches forward in this universe. Events happen in space and time. Right now, I am breathing. That is happening in space and time, though that was previously unnoticed by me and inconsequential to you. Truly, I have also just taken a sip of water. God has seen it. The water slid down my throat. If I stated explicitly that I had *not* taken that sip of water, I would be lying.

This basic construct is critical to establish, because an honest reporting of events often eludes us. The news media in many parts of the world are woefully dishonest. Instead of reporting events, many news media outlets use current events as props to advance an agenda-driven narrative. This results in the devolution of news to propaganda. Lies are told. Even videos are produced, edited, and narrated to give an overall picture that is blatantly untrue. Nearly half a century ago, Dr. Francis Schaeffer demonstrated how the selective editing and dishonest narration of video clips can intentionally mislead an audience.[10]

When we think of propaganda, we may think of Hitler's "Reich Minister of Propaganda," Joseph Goebbels. Or we may think of the former Soviet Union or Communist China. Sadly now, even in the West reliable information is elusive. Most "news" is not a reporting of facts but a weaving together of bits of information to create a pre-ordained narrative. This is nothing less than propaganda. These narratives almost invariably war against objective truth and biblical Christianity.

In many countries, the standard oath of a court witness is, "I promise to tell the truth, the whole truth, and nothing but the truth, so help me God." This oath commits the witness to refrain from weaving a dishonest narrative based on lies or "half-truths." Lamentably, that lofty standard has been replaced by an ends-justify-the-means mentality. Proven liars often go unpunished.

Now Taking Confession

Biblically speaking, honesty and confession are related. They are virtual synonyms. The New Testament term for "confess" is *homo-logeo*, which literally means "same-word." The English term "confess" comes from two Latin roots that similarly connote "with-say." Therefore, the biblical term "confess" means "to say the same thing God is saying."

We ought not to justify or gloss over our sins. Instead, we must confess our sins by saying the same thing God says about them. First John 1:9 instructs us: "If we confess our sins, He is faithful and righteous, so that He will forgive us our sins and cleanse us from all unrighteousness." Here the term *homo-logeo* is used where we read "confess." When we say the same thing that God is saying about our sin, there is a merciful response from God.

This heart-warming verse is surrounded by two corrective verses, 1 John 1:8 and 10, which rebuke dishonesty: "If we *say* that we have no sin, we are deceiving ourselves and the truth is not in us . . . If we *say* that we have not sinned, we make Him a liar and His word is not in us." Instead of using the verb "confess" (*homo-logeo*), the Bible twice uses the word "say" (*lego*). In being untruthful and dishonest, we are not saying the same thing God is saying about our sin. We are not "saying-with" God.

God's remedy for sin is the most important event that happened in the history of the universe. God entered space and time in the form of the Lord Jesus Christ, who was born of the Virgin Mary. He actually died on the cross, in space and time. He rose from the dead, in space and time. Four Gospel writers testify of this narrative. The four Gospel accounts provide very strong evidence. Matthew, Mark, Luke, and John all *confess* that Christ died and rose again. They say what God says about what truly and honestly happened.

To this wonderful event, we also confess unto salvation: "If you *confess* with your mouth Jesus as Lord, and believe in your heart that God raised Him from the dead, you will be saved" (Romans 10:9). In other words, we say the same thing God is saying about Jesus, his Lordship, and his resurrection. That which the Bible says about Jesus' identity and actions are true. We believe this truth, affirm it, and confess it.

The Source of Dishonesty

Various causes of dishonesty exist, such as face-saving measures, avoiding shame, the illegitimate quest for honor, and the desire to triumph in a conflict by any means. Jesus stated unequivocally that that ultimate source of dishonesty is the devil himself.

Obstinate people in Jesus' day thought he was demon-possessed (see Mark 3:22 and John 8:48, 52). Yet, Jesus shed light on this situation as he spoke truth to them:

> *You are of your father the devil, and you want to do the desires of your father. He was a murderer from the beginning, and does not stand in the truth because there is no truth in him. Whenever he tells a lie, he speaks from his own nature, because he is a liar and the father of lies.* —John 8:44

Lying, which is a manifestation of dishonesty, is demonic and sinful. God will not abide this in his presence: "But for the cowardly, and unbelieving, and abominable, and murderers, and sexually immoral persons, and sorcerers, and idolaters, and *all liars*, their part will be in the lake that burns with fire and brimstone, which is the second death" (Revelation 21:8, emphasis added). The Bible places emphasis on the destiny of liars—those who are dishonest without repentance to the extent that their sins come to define their identity.

Honesty in the Movements of New Believers

In our times and contexts, we do well to uphold a high standard of honesty. The Holy Spirit is transforming new believers into the image of Christ. Jesus said, "I am the way, and *the truth*, and the life" (John 14:6). Since we are in Christ, we cannot be immersed in dishonesty. The Holy Spirit is also known as "the Spirit of truth" (John 14:17).

Where dishonesty has occurred, a place remains for repentance. David committed adultery and murder. God forgave David but the psalmist-king still bore the consequences of his actions. David's contrition in Psalm 51 includes this important confession: "Behold, You desire truth in the innermost being" (Psalm 51:6).

Honesty is an internal characteristic. We desire it in our innermost parts—down deep in our hearts. From the overflow of the heart, the mouth speaks. It extends beyond simply a matter of being more careful with our words.

Care must be taken to distinguish between an appropriate level of transparency and honesty, on the one hand, and "too much information (TMI)," on the other. Sometimes TMI manifests as gossip and rumor-spreading, which can devastate church planting and church growth. On other occasions, TMI may create awkward or relationship-rupturing situations because the timing or scope of information may not be appropriate. Honesty should not be equated with blabbing, tattling, or "tell-all" information dumps.

A Word on Honor-Shame Teaching

The new "Honor-Shame" teaching has become popular in missions and cultural anthropology. "Honor-Shame" describes the value system prevalent in many Eastern cultures. In this value system, people act to maximize individual and collective honor and to minimize individual and collective shame.

A full analysis of the Honor-Shame missiology is beyond the scope of this book. However, the Honor-Shame value system tends to promote dishonesty. In other words, when honor is valued over truth, people will lie to avoid shame and disrepute. They will lie to promote their reputation and their family name. Dishonesty requires repentance. We should not expect new Christians or new churches to grow where people value the honor of their name, their family, or their ethnic group above the honor of the Lord Jesus Christ—the Truth.

APPLICATION FOR THE CHURCH TODAY

Jesus as the Truth is the head of the church. The body of Christ must be marked by unwavering honesty. Given the dishonesty that marked Muhammad's paradigm, it is crucially important that the new generation of CMBs remain vigilant regarding dishonesty. I could provide many examples where this has not occurred but such examples would not be edifying. In the West, the virtue and value of honesty have nearly collapsed in the general culture.

While embarrassing and humiliating others should be avoided, we must keep a close personal inventory on honesty. Such internal truthfulness is an essential manifestation of repentance. Repent and believe. Face-saving measures promote a dishonesty that will hinder church growth.

In the long run, integrity will do much to further the move of God. Honesty connects believers by the Spirit of Truth to Jesus. And Jesus is the truth we share with unbelievers. Honesty, marked by straightforwardness, was one secret of the early church's success. The Holy Spirit stamped this DNA on the church from the beginning. Let us be vigilant in upholding that same level of truthfulness today.

FOR FURTHER DISCUSSION

Read Acts 5:1–11.

- According to verse 3, who is the driving force behind all lies?

- What was the impact of the Ananias and Sapphira scandal according to verse 11?

- Do you feel the Holy Spirit's punishment was justified or extreme? Why?

- What are the main sources of dishonesty and untrue narratives in your society?

- What is the relationship between honesty and trust-building among Christians?

CHAPTER 6

FROM PERSECUTOR
TO APOSTLE

G od writes history as the divine storyteller. The true story of Joseph in Genesis stands without parallel even in modern cinema or drama for its suspenseful twists and turns, as well as its ability to evoke emotion from its readers. This chapter features another true story, authored by the divine storyteller. God was not simply content to let the persecution theme in Acts be one of good guys versus bad guys. By his grace, God turned its biggest persecutor into the church's greatest emissary.

The Epitome of the Grace of God: Unmerited Favor

The term *charis* in New Testament Greek is translated as *grace*. The term *grace* has New Testament usages that include "divine enablement": "I labored even more than all of them, yet not I, but the grace of God with me" (1 Corinthians 15:10). Sometimes *charis* is used as *graciousness*: "Your speech must always be with grace, as though seasoned with salt" (Colossians 4:6). But the primary usage of charis/grace in the New Testament signifies

God's unmerited favor toward unworthy humans: "For by grace you have been saved through faith; and this is not of yourselves, it is the gift of God" (Ephesians 2:8). All these verses were penned by Paul, who became a living witness to the grace of God and the gift of salvation.

It seems all humans face formidable enemies. But God is so powerful, no force can match him. Due to this power mismatch, God probably does not view those who oppose him in the same way we view those people and spirits that oppose us. In this chapter, we will see that the fury, self-righteousness, and stubbornness of a Jewish Pharisee named Saul were no match for the grace of God.

God made an example of Saul, later called Paul, to help Christians understand that no situation is truly hopeless. For 2,000 years, Christians have prayed in faith for their persecutors, because Stephen prayed that God would forgive those who were killing him. God answered that prayer by saving one of Stephen's murderers—Saul. Not all persecutors are willing to receive the grace and forgiveness of God—a gift must be received. But one did. And we have much of the Acts narrative and at least 13 of the 27 New Testament books to thank for that fact.

The Road to the Road to Damascus

Saul was a Benjaminite, like his namesake King Saul. He was born not in Israel but in Cilicia in modern-day Turkey. His birthplace was not far from where he would later plant the Galatian churches. Acts 9 records the testimony of Saul's conversion. He also shares his testimony in Acts 22 with a Jewish audience in Jerusalem, and again in Acts 26 while on trial before King Agrippa. He includes biographical information about himself in many of the Pauline epistles. Paul is a historical figure about whom Bible-reading Christians can think his thoughts, feel his feelings, and relive his experiences.

The richness of Saul's life experiences would not go to waste. He was born a Diasporan Jew in Tarsus but he was brought up in Jerusalem. He was taught by the luminary Rabbi Gamaliel. Saul was a Pharisee, a group of people Christians tend to view negatively, given how sharply they opposed Jesus. However, the "Pharisees" were the holiness movement of their day, as their name meant "separated ones." They had helped bring the Jewish people back to God and the law of Moses. Unfortunately, by the time of Jesus' advent, their movement had calcified into an entanglement of rules and traditions that bore the ugly fruit of self-righteousness.

In this context, Saul was born and raised. Though Saul never mentioned seeing Jesus during the Lord's earthly ministry, Saul joined his Pharisaic brethren in persecuting the disciples of Jesus. These disciples were leading many Jews to the new messianic movement based upon a relationship with the risen Savior Jesus. As such, they were a threat to religious leaders who opposed that message.

Saul had a direct hand in the stoning of Stephen. Saul knew how to make tents of leather and animal skin, so looking after overcoats was no challenge for him. But the blood of Stephen did not satisfy Saul's need for justice to be served. Instead, he launched the "great persecution" of Acts 8:1. Inadvertently and ironically, the yet unconverted Saul caused the church's first missionary work among non-Jews! Philip would head off to Samaria, bringing revival there. Over a decade later, God would use Saul, now called Paul, to undertake the church's first intentional cross-cultural missions work.

The Bible portrays Saul as an angry young man. After Steven's death, Luke writes: "Saul began ravaging the church, entering house after house; and he would drag away men and women and put them in prison" (Acts 8:3). Believers in this time could not have enjoyed any freedom of religion, since simply worshipping in one's home could land them in prison.

As I write this in late 2020, Christians in the UK, Canada, Australia, and even the United States—all previously bastions of religious freedom—are facing this dark prospect. These believers are witnessing their legal and constitutionally-guaranteed freedom of religion being rescinded by an arguable rationale regarding public health. In some cases, churches need to work with public officials to promote the common good. Yet, this long after the coronavirus has emerged, and weakened in lethality, such restrictions are persecutorial in nature, especially when gathering places that promote sinful activities are not under the same restrictions.

Turning back to Saul, perhaps his soul was not completely at peace with the savage persecution he was meting out against the disciples of Jesus. The third time Paul recounts his conversion story in Acts, he adds this detail: "And when we had all fallen to the ground, I heard a voice saying to me in the Hebrew dialect, 'Saul, Saul, why are you persecuting Me? It is hard for you to kick against the goads'" (Acts 26:14). Kicking against the goads was an idiom used in those days to illustrate the refusal of a stubborn animal to be prodded in the right direction. This testimonial seems to indicate that the Holy Spirit was convicting Saul of his sins and his persecution campaign against the messianic followers of Jesus. He must have been wrestling internally with this sense of conviction for some time.

The grace and mercy of God flashed to light on the Road to Damascus. God's action in the life of Saul may appear difficult to understand. Such a persecutor of God's people would seem deserving of God's judgment in this lifetime. Nevertheless, God's unmerited favor—the grace of our Lord Jesus Christ—became manifest in and through Paul.

Though Paul would later strike the magician Elymas blind in Paphos for opposing the work of God (Acts 13:11), on the Road to Damascus it was God who would strike blind the persecutor of the church. Saul was so blinded by rage that God needed to temporarily take away his sight so he could speak to him. In this condition, the great persecutor was led by hand into Damascus.

Ananias and Paul: Which One Needed the Other More?

As Christians, we wake up and start our day. For most, that day begins with prayer and devotion, though others may have different rhythms and habits. And don't forget coffee! Then we may go to work or ministry or school or homelife, caring for children or other loved ones. I am a person who appreciates a certain level of predictability. That obsession has caused me more than a little frustration over the years. However, God is sovereign. He knows what is needed in every moment and every day. He can interrupt our plans, and he was about to interrupt the day of a disciple in Damascus named Ananias.

We do not know much about Ananias of Damascus, other than God must have had a high level of confidence in him. Truly this Ananias was a much more trusted disciple than his namesake who fell dead for his dishonesty back in Jerusalem. This Ananias of Damascus experienced a vision about a man temporarily without vision. Yet, Ananias knew the reputation of the man who was the subject of his vision. A chill must have gone down his spine. Luke narrates:

> *Now there was a disciple in Damascus named Ananias; and the Lord said to him in a vision, "Ananias." And he said, "Here I am, Lord." And the Lord said to him, "Get up and go to the street called Straight, and inquire at the house of Judas for a man from Tarsus named Saul, for he is praying, and he has seen in a vision a man named Ananias come in and lay his hands on him, so that he might regain his sight."* —Acts 9:10–12

In Acts, God frequently sent visions to people. The vision God gave Ananias carried a sense of urgency. Ananias could not dodge it. Saul, his soul in the balance, had likewise seen a vision. In it, Ananias would come. If Ananias refused, God could not send Charlie. Still, Ananias hesitated:

> *But Ananias answered, "Lord, I have heard from many people about this man, how much harm he did to Your saints in Jerusalem; and here he has authority from the chief priests to arrest all who call on Your name." But the Lord said to him, "Go, for he is a chosen instrument of Mine, to bear My name before the Gentiles and kings and the sons of Israel; for I will show him how much he must suffer in behalf of My name."* —Acts 9:13–16

At this point, a question arises regarding Saul and Ananias: which one needed the other more? On one hand, the answer would obviously seem to be Saul. He was sitting in a home in Damascus. He had been struck blind. He did not own a seeing-eye dog. His resistance to God seems to have been broken but he did not know what to do next. He needed Ananias if he was to ever see again.

On the other hand, Ananias needed Saul. Sometimes committed Christians need a God-sized task. Emerging churches need a mission field. Faith needs to be challenged and stretched if it is to grow. Such was the situation in which Ananias found himself.

Romanian pastor Richard Wurmbrand continually witnessed to his Communist torturers. He knew that this witness was only likely to increase his misery in this world. Obviously, he was not living for this world.

Returning to Ananias, he was willing to say yes to God. God had said that Saul was his chosen instrument. Interestingly, God had taken the focus off Ananias' potential suffering, by saying of Saul "I will show him how much he must suffer in behalf of My name" (Acts 9:16). Ananias must have shared this part of God's message with Saul. Otherwise, neither Saul nor we would have known about it. The persecutor would become a suffering apostle.

The interaction between Saul and Ananias concluded as follows:

> *So Ananias departed and entered the house, and after laying his hands on him said, "Brother Saul, the Lord Jesus, who appeared to you on the road by which you were coming, has sent me so that you may regain your sight and be filled with the Holy Spirit." And immediately something like fish scales fell from his eyes, and he regained his sight, and he got up and was baptized; and he took food and was strengthened.* —Acts 9:17–19

Ananias did not treat Saul as an untouchable. He laid hands on him. Saul could not see, but Ananias' first words must have been music to his ears: "Brother Saul, the Lord Jesus . . ." By faith, Ananias called Saul his brother, thus welcoming him into the spiritual family of God. They were now brothers in Christ under the care of God their Father. The baptism of Saul must have been an awesome occasion. The baptismal fellowship meal must have been marked by great joy. Due to his faithfulness and obedience, Ananias was able to share in that wonderful fellowship.

Along with Barnabas, Ananias would play a key role in bringing Saul into the family of God, the church. The persecutor would get a new name, Paul. He would begin witnessing for Christ immediately in Damascus. Those who previously partnered with him in persecuting the messianic followers of Jesus soon sought to take his life too. The persecutor had become an apostle. Church history changed forever.

APPLICATION FOR THE CHURCH TODAY

Of all the stories and histories of Acts, the heartwarming testimony of Saul and Ananias is one of the most inspirational. Likewise, this story retains great relevance in these days in which the church of the Lord Jesus Christ faces many persecutors. These persecutors may range from governmental figures to Islamic imams to cyber bullies and online thought police.

The West began its Post-Reformation "train ride" at a stop known as "Christian." Laws, cultures, and worldviews were largely based on a biblical worldview. At worst, they were neutral to the gospel. The Christian consensus among people who were not themselves Christians further encouraged the faith. For example, in many Western nations, Christmas, the holiday marking the birth of the Lord Jesus Christ, is a public holiday.

The Western train moved on from the Christian stop decades ago to another depot some have called "Post-Christian." But that train did not remain long at this depot. The Western train has now reached another stop, "Anti-Christian." The Western church is living in a time when persecution is creeping quickly into the picture. Christian ministry, beliefs, and worldview are disdained among the elites, academia, and in the media. These groups have cast the Bible and prayer out of schools. Christians need strengthening and fortification now, based on faith in Christ and a love for the Word of God. By being alert, the church will be better able to stand.

Contemporary Christians can take heart that some persecutors, like Saul of Tarsus, have come to faith in Christ. Corrie Ten Boom, speaking in a concentration camp to her Nazi persecutors, stated that no one could dig himself a hole so deep that God could not lift him out of it. "Brother Saul" would say "Amen" to that. Let us pray that God would give us a vision for the Sauls of our time.

FOR FURTHER DISCUSSION

Read Acts 9:10–19.

- Which one needed the other more: Saul or Ananias? Why?

- Have you ever had a situation in which you were wary of a new believer? How did the situation work out?

- What types of people do we equate with modern-day Sauls?

- How can fear impact our witness for Christ?

CHAPTER 7

A GOSPEL FOR
THE GENTILES

My father likes to record sporting matches on television and then re-watch them without the commercials. For me, I am too curious; I need to check the result on my cell phone as soon as it happens in real time. Thus, the suspense of watching the recording is broken. I know who will win.

If one were to read the New Testament without knowing an iota of history, two great suspenseful questions would jump off the pages. Since we largely know the answers to these questions now, the suspense has been broken. Nevertheless, suspense is important for holding attention. If we can succeed in putting ourselves back into the Bible story, the way people place themselves into a novel or soap opera, we can regain interest and attention. New insights, previously unseen or glossed over, will appear to us.

The first big suspenseful question in the New Testament was: would Jewish people receive Jesus as their Messiah? The answer was "yes" and "no." Some did; others did not.

This response triggered the second suspenseful question of the New Testament: Would Messianic Jews receive new Gentile followers of Jesus into their new and growing community? The answer would largely be yes. Since we look back from a historical perspective, and since we realize that the vast majority of Christ-worshippers today are Gentiles, this second suspenseful question may seem to have had a foregone conclusion. We should not assume that was so.

Appreciating the Rift Between Jews and Gentiles

Jews considered Gentiles to be pagan, unclean, and unholy. These *goyim*, or nations, were outside the covenant of circumcision. As will be noted in the next chapter, Paul was accused of bringing Gentiles into the sacred temple, thus defiling it. The apostle turned that into an occasion to give a public witness. But, as soon as he mentioned the word "Gentiles," a riot commenced:

> *And when the blood of Your witness Stephen was being shed, I also was standing nearby and approving, and watching over the cloaks of those who were killing him.' And He said to me, 'Go! For I will send you far away to the Gentiles.'" They listened to him up to this statement, and then they raised their voices and said, "Away with such a man from the earth, for he should not be allowed to live!"* —Acts 22:20–22

Such was the animosity Jews held in their hearts toward Gentiles.

This animosity was mutual. Many of the learned Athenians sneered at Paul as he spoke about the God of Israel and his plan of salvation in Christ. In Ephesus, the Gentile worshippers of Artemis were incensed that the apostolic preaching might dethrone this "goddess of the hunt." Luke narrates their apoplectic response to the very presence of a Jewish member of Paul's ministry team:

> *So then, some were shouting one thing and some another, for the assembly was in confusion and the majority did not know for what reason they had come together. Some of the crowd concluded it was Alexander, since the Jews had put him forward; and having motioned with his hand, Alexander was intending to make a defense to the assembly. But when they recognized that he was a Jew, a single outcry arose from them all as they shouted for about two hours, "Great is Artemis of the Ephesians!"*
> —Acts 19:32–34, emphasis added

These two riots illustrate the mutual contempt held between Jews and Gentiles. Yet God was about to bring people from each background together into the family of Christ. This would not prove easy. We know the outcome through historical hindsight but this was the biggest challenge facing the nascent Messianic Jewish community in the book of Acts. The outreach to Gentiles began almost by accident, with another deacon, Philip, reaching out to the Samaritans.

Philip's Mission to the Samaritans

The first group of deacons provided the early church much more than just their original job description of prompt table service. From within this group came the great preacher Stephen, the church's first martyr. Immediately after Stephen's martyrdom, Philip commenced the first major missionary campaign among a non-Jewish people. His ministry took place among the Samaritans, who were a strange mixture of Jewish and Gentile, both in their ethnicity and their religious views. Thus, Jews viewed Samaritans as a mongrel people to be avoided.

The Assyrians, upon conquering the Northern Kingdom of Israel in 722 BC, took many Jewish captives and resettled them in their domains. The Assyrians then resettled non-Jewish people in their place, particularly in Samaria. Some ethnic mixing no doubt occurred over the next seven centuries.

Jesus' compassionate encounter in John 4 with the Samaritan woman illustrates the mixed spiritual views of the Samaritans. The Samaritan woman testified that the Samaritans had their own religious identity, and worshipped on a mountain distinct from Jerusalem, namely, Mount Gerizim. Jesus brought this believing woman to faith in himself. She then began to preach to her kinsfolk.

By the time Philip came to Samaria some years later, the Samaritans were steeped in witchcraft. Simon the Sorcerer held sway over the people. Philip stepped into this context, full of the life of God, preaching Christ and practicing deliverance.

> *Philip went down to the city of Samaria and began proclaiming the Christ to them. The crowds were paying attention with one mind to what was being said by Philip, as they heard and saw the signs which he was performing. For in the case of many who had unclean spirits, they were coming out of them shouting with a loud voice; and many who had been paralyzed or limped on crutches were healed. So there was much rejoicing in that city. —Acts 8:5–8*

Peter and John would later come down to support Philip in establishing the work. Truly, there was much rejoicing in that city, as there has been for 2,000 years wherever the gospel has taken root in human hearts.

Peter and the Gentile Pentecost at Caesarea

Cornelius was a God-fearing Gentile centurion. God chose Cornelius and his family for the occasion of "the Gentile Pentecost" in Acts 10. God needed to orchestrate this unlikely spiritual breakthrough by giving Peter several visions of eating and fellowshipping with the unclean Gentiles. Simultaneously, an angel appeared to Cornelius, commanding him to send for Peter and virtually giving him the street address at which Peter was staying.

On this occasion, the Holy Spirit fell upon those gathered at Cornelius' house in Caesarea. Peter was in mid-sermon at that moment but God decided to wait no longer. This event marked a milestone that Peter could relate to the skeptical brethren at Jerusalem, both immediately thereafter and later at the Jerusalem Council. Behold what manner of love God exhibits in calling for himself a people from every tribe and tongue and nation! And thank God for the courage of evangelists like Philip and Peter in faithfully witnessing about the good news of Jesus.

The Beautiful Work of the Unnamed Apostles in Antioch

I have traveled to over 40 countries of the world. I have worshipped in hundreds of churches—almost every kind of church. In almost all cases, if you ask those "old-timers" in the church, they can tell you who founded the church.

Interestingly, we still do not know the names of the missionaries who started the first great missions-sending church at Antioch. Luke mentions that they were from Cyprus and Cyrene but we are never given their names. Luke traveled frequently with Paul, who was sent out along with Barnabas and Mark by that Antioch church as its first missionaries. Paul had lived in Antioch for a year during those early days of the life of that church. He would have surely personally known these unnamed church planters. However, the Holy Spirit for some reason saw fit to keep their identities anonymous. Luke narrates:

> So then those who were scattered because of the persecution that occurred in connection with Stephen made their way to Phoenicia, Cyprus, and Antioch, speaking the word to no one except to Jews alone. But there were some of them, men of Cyprus and Cyrene, who came to Antioch and began speaking to the Greeks as well, preaching the good news of the Lord Jesus. And the hand of the Lord was with them, and a large number who believed turned to the Lord. —Acts 11:19–21

These brave witnesses preached to Gentiles, resulting in many conversions and a mixed Jewish-Gentile church. We do not know the names of the witnesses who were about to launch the greatest missions movement the world has ever seen. Even today, self-effacing Christian leadership is a sure way to make sure God gets the glory.

What We Can Learn from the Early Missions Teams

God specifically prepared missionary teams to bring the gospel of Christ to the Gentiles. Initially, these teams were made up of

Jewish apostles, though Gentile missionaries were later added to these teams. Teamwork provides vital strength in missions work, as well as in overcoming persecution. The devil's strategy often includes "divide and conquer," which we are unfortunately witnessing in the burdensome pandemic lockdown and confinement regulations of 2020 and 2021.

Luke narrates the ministry of the Antioch-based missionary teams associated with the apostle Paul. Those teams conducted evangelism and church planting ministry, according to Luke's chronology, in Salamis, Paphos, Pisidian Antioch, Iconium, Lycaonia, Lystra, Derbe, Philippi, Thessalonica, Berea, Athens, Corinth, and Ephesus. Space does not allow for a thorough analysis of each ministry initiative. Nevertheless, several overall themes emerge as the gospel crossed over into Gentile communities.

First, encouragement was flowing like a river. The Holy Spirit made a wise choice in coupling Paul with Barnabas for the first missionary trip. Barnabas' real name was Joseph, but the early church gave him the Hebrew name that means "Son of Encouragement." Barnabas' encouragement was largely responsible for Paul becoming a missionary. Immediately after Paul's conversion on the Damascus Road, Barnabas vouched for him before the wary leaders of the Jerusalem church (Acts 9:27). In Antioch, Barnabas could have tried to keep the ministry leadership in his own hands, but he knew Paul had a calling to minister to Gentiles. So, Barnabas left Antioch to search for Paul and bring him from Tarsus.

This type of selflessness and encouragement are critical in missions teamwork. This same encouragement is also greatly needed in our times as the church faces intense persecution.

The devil seeks to discourage. Christians at times face crushing challenges and piercing pain. Every long-standing believer is keenly aware of this. In the face of all this, God seeks to encourage Christians.

Second, miracles were overflowing as the gospel came to the Gentiles. God showed he was stronger than the demonic false-gods and pagan deities that bound the Gentiles. He did so with a mighty display of power that included physical healings and deliverances from demons. In Ephesus, even the demons testified they knew about Paul, the servant of Christ. Today, we should not shrink back in unbelief. Rather, we should continue to pray and believe God for miracles, even as formidable forces of persecution surround us.

Third, teaching and preaching about Jesus were also flowing. The missions teams from Acts 13 onward fulfilled Acts 1:8. Christ's servants were witnessing of him to the uttermost parts of the known world. Paul describes a special revelation the Lord gave him to help shepherd believing Gentiles into the kingdom of God as "fellow heirs and fellow members of the body." As a prisoner in Rome, he had time to think about all that had transpired, and he wrote about it to his disciples in Ephesus:

> For this reason I, Paul, the prisoner of Christ Jesus for the sake of you Gentiles—if indeed you have heard of the administration of God's grace which was given to me for you; that by revelation there was made known to me the mystery, as I wrote before briefly. By referring to this, when you read you can understand my insight into the mystery of Christ, which in other generations was not made known to mankind, as it has now been revealed to His holy apostles and prophets in the Spirit;

to be specific, that the Gentiles are fellow heirs and fellow members of the body, and fellow partakers of the promise in Christ Jesus through the gospel, of which I was made a minister, according to the gift of God's grace which was given to me according to the working of His power. To me, the very least of all saints, this grace was given, to preach to the Gentiles the unfathomable riches of Christ, and to enlighten all people as to what the plan of the mystery is which for ages has been hidden in God, who created all things. —Ephesians 3:1–9

Through the apostles' preaching, Gentiles were able to embrace "the mystery of Christ." The Jewish Messiah became as real to them as he was to his Jewish worshippers. Together, these believers became one unified body. Indeed, many of the early churches in Acts were mixed Jewish-Gentile, flowing in tremendous harmony.

Fourth, the apostles were flexible in their strategy. Generally, Paul and his associates conducted short evangelistic campaigns. However, Paul was not against setting up in a city for a longer length of time to more fully establish a regional work. Luke chronicles the long stays of Paul as follows:

- Antioch: one year (Acts 11:26)
- Corinth: a year and a half (Acts 18:11)
- Ephesus: three years (Acts 20:31)
- Rome: two years, as a prisoner (Acts 28:30)

This strategy caused these cities to become regional centers for the gospel. From there, the gospel spread. For example, Luke describes the impact of Paul's ministry at the School of Tyrannus in

Ephesus: "This took place for two years, so that all who lived in Asia heard the word of the Lord, both Jews and Greeks" (Acts 19:10).

Such flexibility in strategy can also be helpful in times of persecution. In high-persecution contexts, churches may by necessity meet in small groups or home meetings. Inflexibility can become a hindrance both in missions work and in church function during times of persecution.

The Jerusalem Council: An Example of Peaceably Working Out Divisions in the Church

The early church was not without its internal problems. Indeed, all human relationships include some conflict. Paul and Barnabas had a sharp argument before the second missionary trip regarding whether to give John Mark a second chance on the mission field. Their monumental Galatian revivals were nearly undone by legalistic teachers who came in afterward and contradicted Paul's teaching. Paul began his corrective letter to the Galatians with an ominous reference to "this present evil age": "Grace to you and peace from God the Father and our Lord Jesus Christ, who gave Himself for our sins so that He might rescue us from *this present evil age*" (Galatians 1:3–4, emphasis added). Indeed, rampant immorality and divisions gripped the church in Corinth, even after Paul had taught there for a year and a half.

As stated above, the biggest challenge facing the early church in Acts was incorporating the Gentiles into Christ's Kingdom. By God's help, they were able to do so. The Jerusalem Council of Acts 15 illustrates conflict resolution in the church. The leaders were in mutual submission to each other. They reached a reasonable resolution relying heavily on Old Testament Scriptures. Apparently, the listeners were greatly moved by the testimonies of Paul and Barnabas regarding the miracles God had wrought among the Gentiles (Acts 15:12). These testimonials confirmed to them that God was concerned for the salvation of Gentiles.

APPLICATION FOR THE CHURCH TODAY

We must continue witnessing for Christ even in the face of persecution. Neither should we cease our missions efforts due to hostility. Many people groups still await the gospel. Muslims, Hindus, Buddhists, and Animists may seem as "foreign" to the Christian faith as the Gentiles were to messianic Judaism. The Holy Spirit continues to empower Christians to witness of Christ among the nations.

Whenever the gospel enters a people group for the first time, persecution ensues. Most of this resistance can be attributed to spiritual warfare. Demonic powers do not want to relinquish their control easily. However, they cannot stand against the power of the Holy Spirit. That was true during the book of Acts, and it is true today.

The Acts of the Apostles provides several important lessons today as we continue to bring the gospel to the lost. Teamwork remains vital. Encouragement is underestimated but it can be a "game-changer." We continue to believe God for signs and wonders. He works miracles still. Finally, Christians should not be locked into any one methodology. Those may work in one place and one time but even the apostles showed flexibility in their strategies. Today is still a day of harvest among both Jews and Gentiles. In conclusion, Paul testified: "I am not ashamed of the gospel, for it is the power of God for salvation to everyone who believes, to the Jew first and also to the Greek" (Romans 1:16). Peace to all.

FOR FURTHER DISCUSSION

Read Acts 15:19–20.

- What things did Gentiles need to leave behind to follow Christ and to enter into open fellowship with other believers?

- In what ways may our traditions and suspicions "cause trouble" to unbelievers who are turning to God?

- What guidelines, if any, would you recommend for new church members in your context? Why?

CHAPTER 8

MISREPRESENTED!

The apostle Paul presents an amazing example of the grace of God in action. For 2,000 years, Christians have studied the life of Paul and read his epistles. Christian theologians have never tired of trying to figure out Paul. My wife and I named our youngest son Paul.

Paul the Benjaminite was a "Hebrew of Hebrews" (Philippians 3:5). He was a Pharisee and an expert in Jewish law. Nonetheless, God called this man to be an apostle to the Gentiles. Sometimes God calls people to minister in contexts outside the area of their natural expertise. We do well to embrace this ourselves and encourage others to pursue God's call if he has given them such an unexpected call.

The missions teams led by Paul, Barnabas, Silas, and Timothy proved a tremendous success. Gentiles poured into the kingdom of God. Other than the imperial city of Rome itself, it seemed the biggest missions challenge for the early church would be the great pagan city of Ephesus. In Acts 18, Apollos ministered there, bolstered by Priscilla and Aquila. Acts 19 chronicles Paul's arrival and the ensuing revival. As mentioned in the previous chapter, Paul spent two years teaching in Ephesus at the School of Tyrannus. The word of God spread throughout that whole region (Acts 19:9–10).

Paul's Road Back to Jerusalem

Paul was a visionary. He had appealed to go to Rome. He had visions of ministry in Spain. Yet, while in Ephesus, the great Apostle to the Gentiles curiously began to speak of returning to Jerusalem: "Now after these things were finished, Paul resolved in the Spirit to go to Jerusalem after he had passed through Macedonia and Achaia, saying, 'After I have been there, I must also see Rome'" (Acts 19:21).

The language used here, "in the Spirit," indicates that Paul was not simply homesick for Jewish contexts. Shortly thereafter, Paul bade farewell to the Ephesian elders. Luke chronicles Paul's urgency to return to Jerusalem: "For Paul had decided to sail past Ephesus so that he would not have to lose time in Asia; for he was hurrying, if it might be possible for him to be in Jerusalem the day of Pentecost" (Acts 20:16).

Paul told the Ephesian elders that they would never see his face again. They must have surely concluded that their mentor would be slain in Jerusalem. Yet, Paul used very strong language about his mission to Jerusalem. He stated he had no choice in the matter. The Spirit compelled him to go. The phrase in the following passage can be translated as "bound by the Holy Spirit" or "bound in spirit." That is, Paul felt compelled to go:

> *And now, behold,* bound by the Spirit, *I am on my way to Jerusalem, not knowing what will happen to me there, except that the Holy Spirit solemnly testifies to me in every city, saying that chains and afflictions await me.*
> —Acts 20:22–23, emphasis added

Sometimes the Holy Spirit gives us a choice of options. At times God simply allows us to use our sanctified minds and faculties to make the best decision possible. Sometimes Christians pray and God provides guidance. But there are some occasions where the compulsion of God is very strong. We have no choice but to obey. God knows best and he knows what will happen next. Believers must trust and obey.

As Paul got nearer to Jerusalem, the tension and suspense increased. Philip and his family hosted Paul in Caesarea, where Philip had settled after the Samaritan revival. In this city, Paul would stand as a free man. Later, he would return to Caesarea in chains. Luke reports first-hand that a prophet urgently warned Paul not to go to Jerusalem:

> *As we were staying there for some days, a prophet named Agabus came down from Judea. And he came to us and took Paul's belt and bound his own feet and hands, and said, "This is what the Holy Spirit says: 'In this way the Jews in Jerusalem will bind the man who owns this belt and hand him over to the Gentiles.'" When we had heard this, we as well as the local residents began begging him not to go up to Jerusalem. Then Paul replied, "What are you doing, weeping and breaking my heart? For I am ready not only to be bound, but even to die in Jerusalem for the name of the Lord Jesus." And since he would not be persuaded, we became quiet, remarking, "The will of the Lord be done!"* —Acts 21:10–14

Something or someone appeared to be driving Paul to Jerusalem. This passage indicates it was the Spirit of God leading Paul there to give testimony to the name of the Lord Jesus. That single testimony would change Paul's life forever.

Misrepresented by Believers

I am a person that likes things to go smoothly in ministry. Since I am in ministry to Muslims, that rarely happens. Plan A seldom happens. Most of ministry is Plan B and Plan C. In the end, it seems better not to have much of a plan at all, since this impedes flexibility and may end in frustration.

Paul's epic and consequential journey to the holy city finally ended with the apostle arriving in Jerusalem. Things did not go smoothly from the beginning. In Acts 15, Paul had come to the Jerusalem Council and testified what God was doing among the Gentiles. He did so once again as he became reacquainted with James and the other leaders of the Jerusalem church. Luke narrates:

> *After we arrived in Jerusalem, the brothers and sisters received us gladly. And the following day Paul went in with us to James, and all the elders were present. After he had greeted them, he began to relate one by one the things which God had done among the Gentiles through his ministry. And when they heard about them, they began glorifying God."* —Acts 21:17–20

So far, so good. And Paul no doubt rejoiced to hear that the messianic message was growing fast among the Jews of Jerusalem: "And they said to him, "You see, brother, how many thousands there are among the Jews of those who have believed, and they are all zealous for the Law . . ." (Acts 21:20). So far, so good, it seemed.

At this point, within that same sentence, a pivot occurred in the narrative. These great and godly leaders reported the first misrepresentation of Paul. And it seems they half believed it:

". . . and they have been told about you, that you are teaching all the Jews who are among the Gentiles to abandon Moses, telling them not to circumcise their children nor to walk according to the customs." —Acts 21:21

A communication breakdown had occurred. Perhaps it was vicious rumors. Maybe it was innocent miscommunication. Paul had told Gentiles they did not need to be circumcised, lest they be obliged to keep the entire law. His message was directed to the Gentiles, noting what aspects of the law were important to keep, such as abstaining from sexual immorality, and which were not. These leaders had previously commissioned Paul at the Jerusalem Council to communicate their decisions to the Gentiles. Beginning with the second missionary journey with Silas, Paul had faithfully done so.

Now, Paul was being misrepresented. Paul did not teach Jews to forsake Moses, as was being reported. It appears the believers were confused about him. They did not urge him simply to disregard this as a rumor. Instead, they said:

So what is to be done? They will certainly hear that you have come. Therefore, do as we tell you: we have four men who have a vow upon themselves; take them along and purify yourself together with them, and pay their expenses so that they may shave their heads; and then everyone will know that there is nothing to what they have been told about you, but that you yourself also conform, keeping the Law. —Acts 20:22-24

Paul submitted to the leaders of the Jerusalem church. Perhaps he was planning to undergo ritual purification anyway if he had been planning to go to the temple.

Believers today must be careful in receiving reports about other believers. Paul would later receive and believe a report about the Corinthians from a trusted source: "For I have been informed concerning you, my brothers and sisters, by Chloe's people, that there are quarrels among you" (1 Corinthians 1:11). Paul acted on this information by penning a corrective letter, 1 Corinthians.

Too often, however, Christians receive reports about other brothers and sisters of like-precious faith in Christ without giving such reports proper scrutiny. Many times, these reports contain twisted information. Or a kernel of truth may be used to construct a castle of untruth. Facts—bits of information that are individually correct—may be arranged such that the overall story is untrue. Aaron tried this in explaining the origin of the Golden Calf. He conveniently left out his own role in the abominable project!

The sources that seek to defame Christians are often evil in origin; they would like nothing more than seeing Christians divided. A story has circulated of five pastors who were arrested in Czechoslovakia during the Communist period. Each of the five was individually interrogated by the Communist officials, who made up lies about what the other pastors said about him. To a man, they replied, "My brother would never have said that about me. Even if he did, I will forgive him." These replies even moved their Communist captors. What a testimony. As days of persecution amplify worldwide, be careful, little ears, what you hear. And be careful, little hearts, what you believe.

Misrepresented by Unbelievers

One must give credit to Paul. Had I been in Paul's shoes, after that rocky start with the believers in Jerusalem, I would have booked the next trip out of town. Yet, Paul was compelled to stay to witness for Christ. He was willing to endure some misrepresentation at the hands of believers who had received twisted information about him.

The treatment of Paul by the brethren was minor compared to the treatment he would receive at the hands of unbelievers. The problem began with another misrepresentation, this time malicious:

> *Then Paul took along the men, and the next day, after purifying himself together with them, he went into the temple giving notice of the completion of the days of purification, until the sacrifice was offered for each one of them. When the seven days were almost over, the Jews from Asia, upon seeing him in the temple, began to stir up all the crowd and laid hands on him, crying out, "Men of Israel, help! This is the man who instructs everyone everywhere against our people and the Law and this place; and besides, he has even brought Greeks into the temple and has defiled this holy place!" For they had previously seen Trophimus the Ephesian in the city with him,* and they thought *that Paul had brought him into the temple.* —Acts 21:26–29, emphasis added

The earlier confusion persisted about what Paul actually taught regarding the law and the temple. The malice manifested with a false report of Paul defiling the temple with Gentiles. Luke narrates that this malicious misrepresentation was based on a convenient alibi—the sighting of Trophimus with Paul.

This malicious representation resulted in Paul receiving a vicious beating. It looked as if the end was near:

> *Then the whole city was provoked and the people rushed together, and taking hold of Paul they dragged him out of the temple, and immediately the doors were shut. While they were intent on killing him, a report came up to the commander of the Roman cohort that all Jerusalem was in confusion. He immediately took along some soldiers and centurions and ran down to the crowd; and when they saw the commander and the soldiers, they stopped beating Paul.* —Acts 21:30–32

The intervention of the Roman cohort spared Paul's life. It would not have taken long for a mob to kill a man under such circumstances. Paul would be persecuted by the very same spirit by which he had previously persecuted Christians. He intimately knew the context, and he would not give up.

The concluding section of this chapter addresses the two-millennia challenge of Christians being misrepresented by unbelievers. However, now we will focus on the climax of Paul's story. His purpose for coming to Jerusalem was drawing near. He was willing to deal with misrepresentation as a part of the persecuted church.

Misrepresented by "Crazies"

Paul's trip to Jerusalem was going poorly by many standards. He had been misrepresented by believers. Then he was misrepresented by unbelievers and beaten nearly to death. However, the content of these accusations and misrepresentations was still in the realm of the credible. This content focused on Jewish law, the holiness of the temple, Gentile conversion, and ceremonial purification. All of these were common themes in Paul's preaching and writing.

Soon, the content would turn to the absurd. Paul, beaten and bleeding, no doubt stretched to his physical limit, would next be confronted with lunacy:

> *As Paul was about to be brought into the barracks, he said to the commander, "May I say something to you?" And he said, "Do you know Greek? Then you are not the Egyptian who some time ago stirred up a revolt and led the four thousand men of the Assassins out into the wilderness?"* —Acts 21:37–38

This misrepresentation by the Roman commander appeared to come out of nowhere. He mistook Paul as an Egyptian terrorist. Where did he ever get this idea? Were such rumors swirling in the Roman ranks? It does not seem credible that a Jewish evangelist would closely resemble in comportment an Egyptian terrorist, but these were crazy times.

Once again, Paul did not quit. But Paul pressed through all this persecution and misrepresentation. He was not sidetracked. The real purpose of this long journey had come:

> *But Paul said, "I am a Jew of Tarsus in Cilicia, a citizen of no insignificant city; and I beg you, allow me to speak to the people." When he had given him permission, Paul, standing on the stairs, motioned to the people with his hand; and when there was a great silence, he spoke to them in the Hebrew dialect.* —Acts 21:39–40

Paul endured it all for the witness of Christ! At this point, he launched into a testimony that kept his Jewish listeners enraptured. He was able to witness for his Lord Jesus in the city that earlier put him on the cross.

Paul leaves us a tremendous example of enduring misrepresentation for the sake of the gospel. He could easily have gotten frustrated to the point of exploding. He could have quit. Yet, he persevered for the sake of the witness. That day was Paul's last day as a free man, but he must have felt truly free, having discharged the burden of the Lord. The witness continued and the church continued to grow.

APPLICATION FOR THE CHURCH TODAY
When the Church is Misrepresented by Propaganda
Paul overcame lies and misrepresentation. His epistles live on. Those rumors against him have largely faded away.

For 2,000 years, the church of the Lord Jesus has often found itself growing in the thorny soil of persecution. In such contexts, powers unsympathetic to the church control the news and narratives. In the early days, the church's "love feasts" (Jude 12) were misrepresented as orgies. In the former Soviet Union, Christians were reported by the Marxist media to sacrifice children. In Muslim contexts, Christians are regularly slandered as immoral people.

In many cases, such as in the former Soviet Union, Christians had no public media by which to counter false narratives and malicious misrepresentations. Today, in the era of "fake news," innocent young people are unwittingly drawn into an electronic noose in which good is called evil and evil is called good. Christians are deemed hypocrites. Hollywood often portrays Christian ministers as evil predators.

The battle against misrepresentation and fake news may prove more wearying to Christians than blows on the back. Overcoming such misrepresentation can be an exhausting endeavor. Today, we live in a propagandist era with the social media giants such as Google, Twitter, and Facebook increasingly hostile to the church and Christian values. Simply stating a biblical value or preaching the gospel can be deemed hate speech, resulting in fines or imprisonment. The social media giants, likewise, may censor, de-platform, or de-monetize Christian values and beliefs. Pastor Andrew Brunson, who was imprisoned in Turkey, foresees that de-platforming may make it difficult for churches to get their message out, or even to maintain a public website.[11]

In these days, the church must remain strong. Believers understand that in eternity every evil lie will be revealed. We may not be able to restore all the damage done to those who have been spiritually injured and deceived by propaganda and misrepresentation, but those lies will ultimately end. Jesus, the Truth, will live forever. And believers in Christ will live forever with him.

In the meantime, we must be careful regarding our news sources. Understand that part of the propaganda in the spirit of anti-Christ is to misrepresent Christians so they will turn against each other. Paul said he was not unaware of the devil's schemes. Let us be likewise alert and vigilant. For in doing so, we will be ready to testify to the grace of our Lord Jesus.

FOR FURTHER DISCUSSION

Read Acts 21:27–32.

- How was Paul misrepresented by unbelievers and why do you think they did that?

- How did he respond?

- What are the main channels or voices through which Christians are misrepresented today?

- How should we respond?

- How can we help our children and new believers receive accurate teaching, education, and input in these trying times?

CHAPTER 9

LEGAL TRIALS

Legal entanglements were not unknown to Paul. As Saul, he dragged the followers of Messiah Jesus into prison. After God called and saved him, Paul found himself in prison overnight in Philippi in Acts 16. In Acts 18, Paul's riotous opponents in Corinth dragged him before the Roman proconsul Gallio, who promptly dismissed the case. And in Acts 19 at Ephesus, another riot broke out by those who opposed the preaching of Jesus. Here, the Ephesian town clerk stepped in to play the calming role of Gamaliel. He encouraged the rioters to bring a legal court case against Paul if they had one. But they did not.

These legal entanglements, detainments, and imprisonments proved to be short-term. At the end of Acts 21, the legal situation changed. Paul's Jewish opponents committed themselves to kill Paul at all costs. The Roman authorities had not delegated to their Jewish subjects the authority to execute criminals. The Jewish nation, as an occupied people, could only recommend that the Romans execute the accused. In the case of Jesus, they were able to successfully elicit a Roman execution decision. With Paul, they were unable to do so. On one hand, the Roman authorities shielded Paul from a sure, swift, and bloody death at the hands of the mob. On the other hand, Paul would never again be a free man in the annals of the Acts narrative. The Acts of the Apostles ends with Paul imprisoned in Rome.

This chapter considers the legal trials of Paul the prisoner. Like so many Christians who would follow after him, Paul served Christ while in chains. He testified: "I am wearing this chain for the sake of the hope of Israel" (Acts 28:20). Paul did not feel sorry for himself. Paul's experiences provide many insights into God's concern for those behind bars for the name of Jesus.

Paul Becomes a Prisoner

The previous chapter addressed the misrepresentations of Paul. He endured all those misrepresentations for the sake of witnessing to Christ to his Jewish brethren. Prior to his great testimonial narrated in Acts 22, the mob beat him badly. He would have been killed by them had it not been for the quick intervention of the Roman commander. Nevertheless, the commander took Paul into custody in Acts 21:33.

Twenty-one of Acts' 28 chapters lie behind us. A full one-quarter of the book of Acts remains ahead. But Paul had become a prisoner and would remain so until the end of the book. The Holy Spirit therefore committed one-quarter of the only inspired family history of the early church to the trials of one prisoner. The other apostles had launched into ministry in far-flung places. They would also encounter chains and death for the name of the Lord Jesus. However, to encourage and teach those who would later wear chains for Christ, and seemingly as an early tribute to them, the Holy Spirit inspired Luke to dedicate so much material to describing the plight and perseverance of one solitary prisoner.

What Should Christians Use to Their Legal Advantage?

This is a difficult question for which space does not allow an in-depth treatment. We observe, nonetheless, that Paul took advantage of two "identities." The first was his identity as a Roman citizen. Rome maintained a two-tiered system of status. Roman citizens were in the first tier. They enjoyed certain rights, such as not being beaten without a trial. Paul "plays this card" at the end of his brief imprisonment in Philippi in Acts 16. Interestingly, he did not bring up that citizenship in Philippi prior to his brief imprisonment.

He mentioned his Roman citizenship again in Acts 22. The Romans rescued him from being torn apart after his public testimony. The Romans had a policy of "blaming the victim." They would give a preliminary beating or whipping to anyone around whom a disturbance arose. Luke narrates this riot:

> *The commander ordered that he be brought into the barracks, saying that he was to be interrogated by flogging so that he would find out the reason why they were shouting against him that way. But when they stretched him out with straps, Paul said to the centurion who was standing by, "Is it lawful for you to flog a man who is a Roman and uncondemned?"* —Acts 22:24–25

Paul appeared almost nonchalant about the whipping and his subsequent explanation of his Roman citizenship. Paul's remarkable composure would have made for fascinating theater to watch live.

Paul's Roman identity statement provided him partial protection, though it did not spare him the agonies of being a prisoner. Paul used his citizenship again to appeal to Caesar. Ultimately, to Caesar in Rome he would go.

The second identity Paul utilized in his legal trials was that of being a Pharisee. The Roman commander brought Paul to be tried by the Sanhedrin. Most of the Council members were eager to have Paul put to death. Paul had only uttered one sentence when the high priest ordered him to be struck on the mouth (Acts 23:2). Tensions were already high and escalating.

Essentially, this was a kangaroo court designed to condemn the one they considered to be an apostate and a traitor. Those who have stood before rigged trials in Communist lands can empathize with the hopelessness of Paul's situation. Those charged with apostasy in Muslim lands, trapped between the hammer of evil laws and the anvil of evil and impatient judges, can likewise understand the plight of Paul the prisoner.

Then, a stunning reversal occurred in that trial before the Sanhedrin:

> But Paul, perceiving that one group were Sadducees and the other Pharisees, began crying out in the Council, "Brothers, I am a Pharisee, a son of Pharisees; I am on trial for the hope and resurrection of the dead!" When he said this, a dissension occurred between the Pharisees and Sadducees, and the assembly was divided. For the Sadducees say that there is no resurrection, nor an angel, nor a spirit, but the Pharisees acknowledge them all. And a great uproar occurred; and some of the scribes of the Pharisaic party stood up and started arguing heatedly, saying, "We find nothing wrong with this man; suppose a spirit or an angel has spoken to him?" —Acts 23:6–9

Paul's strategy worked brilliantly. Luke does not indicate if Paul had given any forethought to using this wedge tactic. It is likely he knew these people so well that the Holy Spirit merely gave him the insight to speak of resurrection at the needed time. Whatever the details, this usage of his Pharisaic identity brought some of Paul's adversaries around to this defense.

Paul's example illustrates that Christians can utilize the legal resources available. Paul used his rights as a Roman citizen to appeal to Caesar. He utilized his identity as a Pharisee when doing so was appropriate. He used the identities God gave him *not to escape suffering but to enable his witness for Christ*. I believe this is a key distinction. If God provides resources to further our witness, we can use those resources should he lead us that way.

At other times, family relationships may provide conflicts and entanglements. John 18:15 indicates that the apostle John knew Caiaphas the high priest. He could have tried to leverage that relationship to get Jesus out of trouble. Such a political maneuver would have been contrary to the plan of God! However, John never allowed that relationship with Caiaphas, who opposed Jesus, to pull him away from Christ. May we sanctify Christ in our hearts and, like John and Paul, make decisions that glorify Jesus.

Nearly Torn Limb from Limb

The division in the Sanhedrin resulted in confusion that ended the trial. But as soon as the trial broke up, a riot broke out. The presiding Roman commander was accustomed to observing violence. His troops were doubtless experts in administering physical punishment. He must have credibly thought Paul was going to be torn limb from limb, which is not a pleasant way to leave this world.

And when a great dissension occurred, the commander
was afraid that Paul would be torn to pieces *by them,*
and he ordered the troops to go down and take him away
from them by force, and bring him into the barracks.
—Acts 23:10, emphasis added

God used the Roman commander to rescue Paul. By the
end of Acts, it seems no small miracle that Paul was still alive.
Forty assassins had sworn they would neither eat nor drink until
they had slain Paul. We do not know if they starved to death, if
they reneged on their vow, or if they were given some type of
religious exemption or dispensation to eat and drink again.

Sketching Out Paul's Trials Before Lysias, Felix, Festus, and Agrippa

Acts chapters 24 through 26 narrate Paul's trials before four Roman
governors and magistrates. He encountered various challenges.
Paul's Jewish opponents utilized a sweet-talking lawyer named
Tertullus who tried to curry favor with Governor Felix.

When Christian prisoners go on trial, "politics" often occur
behind the scenes. When Jesus was condemned to death, Herod
and Pilate at last became friends (Luke 23:12). In a political
gesture, Pilate released Barabbas to those Jews who opposed
Jesus. After Herod executed James and, when he saw that it
pleased that same faction, he arrested Peter (Acts 12:3).

The situation repeated itself with Paul. Felix "wanting to do
the Jews a favor" left Paul in prison (Acts 24:27). Likewise, during
Paul's next trial, Festus wanted to do the Jews a favor by allowing
them to kill Paul (Acts 25:9). Sadly, the Jewish religious leadership
that opposed Jesus had become politicians and ceased being

spiritual leaders. Perhaps this was part of the reason they did not recognize their promised messiah, the non-political Jesus.

Paul on the defense stand presented a stark contrast to the typical, scheming politician. He was resolute, yet gracious. He even applauded the hope in God cherished by his accusers (Acts 24:15). A temptation may arise to respond to nastiness with nastiness. Social media provides a seemingly perfect platform for such nastiness or sarcasm. Yet, let us glorify God and remain gracious as Paul was. Gracious but firm.

Paul stood before Roman officials who knew the issues regarding Jewish law and Jesus, as well as others who were clueless about these issues. Gallio in Corinth refused to even hear anything about Jewish laws, names, and controversies. Likewise, Claudius Lysias acknowledged his unfamiliarity with these Jewish spiritual issues when he wrote to Felix (Acts 23:29). Yet he at least knew these religious questions were not capital offenses according to Roman law.

Paul stood before Felix who had a "quite accurate knowledge about the Way" (Acts 24:22) Since Felix was a political schemer, that accurate knowledge did not benefit Paul. Paul likewise stood before King Agrippa, who was well informed about Jewish issues, as reflected in Paul's opening statement:

> *Regarding all the things of which I am accused by the Jews, King Agrippa, I consider myself fortunate that I am about to make my defense before you today, especially because you are an expert in all customs and questions among the Jews; therefore I beg you to listen to me patiently.* —Acts 26:2–3

Interestingly, Paul followed this opening with his personal testimony. As always, Paul took every opportunity to glorify Jesus. He was less concerned with his own defense or vindication. What a lesson for believers in Christ who find themselves on trial in these times. It would certainly be human nature to try to defend ourselves. However, God may provide a unique opportunity to glorify his name. Christians who are not self-absorbed will more easily recognize these opportunities.

Christians Must Fight Their Way Out of Spiritual Ambushes

Paul's opponents tried to manipulate the legal system. Their goal was to set up a transport situation in which they could ambush Paul and slay him. God providentially allowed Paul's nephew to overhear an early form of this plan (Acts 23:16). Later, when Paul was imprisoned in Caesarea, Paul's opponents tried again to set up a lethal ambush. Festus became complicit in the plan to send Paul back to Jerusalem, where he would have been ambushed and killed on the way (Acts 25:3). Paul wisely insisted on his right to appeal to Caesar in Rome, avoiding a near-certain death on the road back to Jerusalem.

At times, Muslim persecutors of Christians frame them in a situation so they may accuse them of breaking blasphemy laws. At times, unbelievers produce false witnesses to catch Christians in a legal ambush. In such situations, many Christians have joined the company of Christ's martyrs.

We can apply the principles of ambush to our lives. Paul persevered in the face of spiritual, legal, and physical ambush. Ambush is a common military strategy that involves deception— it is a normal part of warfare. When a military unit is ambushed, they must fight their way out of the ambush. Hopefully, help will arrive. But they cannot panic and freeze, waiting to be annihilated.

Spiritually, we cannot panic if we are ambushed by persecution. We must continue fighting in prayer—our enemies are not flesh and blood. We must also continue looking for every opportunity to witness. Our faith in Christ must not waver. We must stand and fight on.

God's Help to Prisoners

The Reverend Terry Waite was an Anglican Church envoy who spent four years as a hostage held by Islamic terrorists in Lebanon. Reverend Waite was kept blindfolded, which is a cruel and disorienting form of punishment that deprives the captive of the normal visual clues needed to retain one's orientation and sanity. Reverend Waite testified that he could see three little pinpricks on the wall, just visible under his blindfold. He beheld those three pinpricks and meditated on Father, Son, and Holy Spirit. This is one modern example of how God can sustain his servants in the midst of imprisonment. God may use different means but he is able to strengthen those who suffer for his name.

God Strengthens Paul Through Night Visions

The Bible paints a picture of Paul as a resolute and mature servant of Christ. Christ appeared to Paul personally and gave him personal revelations. Paul had also ascended by vision into the third heaven (2 Corinthians 12:2). In many ways, Paul appears to surpass us, the ordinary believers.

However, Paul was human. He was beset by emotional fears and physical weaknesses. Paul was always strategizing future ministry in "regions beyond," "where Christ was not known." He talked of a pioneer mission to Spain (Romans 15:24). Though he clearly felt compelled to testify of Jesus in Jerusalem, it is unlikely that he knew he would subsequently lose all freedom to travel in ministry. Could he have ever experienced loneliness, frustration, and despair? Certainly, he could have.

God frequently utilized night visions to encourage Paul the prisoner. These visions always included a word from the Lord that assured Paul of the outcome in the midst of trials. Luke chronicles at least three such instances in Acts.

First, the opening of this chapter mentioned Paul's brief trial in Corinth. The persecution in Corinth must have been intense, for God needed to reassure the normally unflappable apostle: "And the Lord said to Paul by a vision at night, 'Do not be afraid any longer, but go on speaking and do not be silent; for I am with you, and no one will attack you to harm you, for I have many people in this city'" (Acts 18:9–10). This vision provided the encouragement for Paul to settle in Corinth for a year and a half to develop a deep work there in the midst of a cauldron of paganism and debauchery.

Second, God gave Paul a similar night vision after the apostle had nearly been killed at the Sanhedrin trial: "But on the following night, the Lord stood near him and said, 'Be courageous! For as you have testified to the truth about Me in Jerusalem, so you must testify in Rome also'" (Acts 23:11). Again, the Lord called for courage! This word also gave Paul the guidance needed, and perhaps directed him to later make his appeal to Caesar.

Third, God gave Paul another night vision during the life-and-death shipwreck journey that ended on the shores of Malta. Paul allowed his cup of encouragement to overflow, strengthening even unbelievers in a dire, dark situation. These men had given up all hope of life but Paul told them with certainty:

> *For this very night an angel of the God to whom I belong, whom I also serve, came to me, saying, "Do not be afraid, Paul; you must stand before Caesar; and behold, God has graciously granted you all those who are sailing with you." Therefore, keep up your courage, men, for I believe God that it will turn out exactly as I have been told.*
> —Acts 27:23–25

For a third time, the Scriptures indicate that Paul was afraid and that God sent a word to him via a night vision or an angelic night visitation. To God be the glory. Let us remember and pray for the Lord's prisoners as Hebrews commands: "Remember the prisoners, as though in prison with them, and those who are badly treated, since you yourselves also are in the body" (Hebrews 13:3).

APPLICATION FOR THE CHURCH TODAY
Neither Freedom nor Prison Is Our Ultimate Destination: Heaven Is!

Legal entanglements are a form of persecution that seeks to slow or stop the work of God. Paul's opponents wanted to kill him. Short of that, they sought to stop his effectiveness in the ministry. Though Paul did find himself in chains for Christ, he continued his ministry in Malta and then Rome. From Rome, he wrote the Prison Epistles and continued to minister to visitors.

Today, those who oppose the gospel still use legal entanglements to try to stop the work of God. One form of legal harassment in use today but not in New Testament times is assessing monetary fines on pastors and churches. Frequently, insufficient money is available for legal expenses. Though not mentioned as a form of persecution in Acts, monetary fines often accompany legal entanglements today. Even now, fining Christians, churches and ministers is a way of closing their buildings and suppressing their witness. While I have personally witnessed this tactic in places such as Uzbekistan and Cuba, this same tactic is coming to Western nations whose governments are constitutionally required to protect freedom of religion. Instead, they restrict it.

When I served with a media ministry in the Middle East, one Arab country tended to block Christian media projects by imposing an exorbitant approval fee (known as *baksheesh*). Any Christian ministry would need these approval "stamps" to legally distribute their videos. And they needed approval prior to production as well as after production. In this country, the Muslim officials charged exorbitant *baksheesh* to block projects without actually stating they were blocking the project based on content. However, the Muslim censorship officials liked the Christian videos, especially children's videos which they gave to their own children. So, they began charging videos instead of money as *baksheesh*, which this partner ministry joyfully provided!

In the West, punitive fines are increasingly levied for preaching on certain "cultural" themes, such as homosexuality, or violating onerous governmental regulations. The coronavirus pandemic has provided a covering for those seeking to restrict religious gatherings by declaring them non-essential. However, church services are essential services. The Bible states, "let's consider how to encourage one another in love and good deeds, not abandoning our own meeting together" (Hebrews 10:24–25). Christians are commanded to meet together with other believers. To not do so is a violation of a biblical command, as well as an invitation to discouragement.

When I was in Uzbekistan about a decade ago, I observed how the government there utilized detainments and interrogations to intimidate pastors. These pastors were then fined exorbitant amounts of money, in the hopes that they would be cut off from doing the work of God. This reality created suffering for the pastors and their families. Nevertheless, these pastors persevered and overcame. I also recall standing in the customs line to leave the country, when two government officials summoned me and my colleague from near the back of the line for questioning in a private room. I was thankful to eventually leave the country safely, but I left knowing that brothers and sisters were suffering for their faith.

This chapter concludes by noting that the disciples of Jesus focused on heaven, not on this life alone. Their hope of spending eternity with Jesus made them courageous in the face of death. It was this same hope that they preached to Jewish and Gentile audiences. Jesus died on the cross for the sins of mankind, then he ascended to heaven. The Lord of Lords promised them he was going to prepare a place for all who believe in him.

For these reasons, our goal in days of persecution should be our witness of salvation in Christ. Christ loves sinners, including persecutors. The worst persecutor of the early church became its foremost apostle, before also becoming a prisoner himself. Paul's focus was an eternity. He had his priorities correct. He told his friends in Philippi, those who had seen him in jail there, "For to me, to live is Christ, and to die is gain" (Philippians 1:21). The devil found no foothold in Paul to leverage a fear of death.

Paul's goal was to witness of Christ. His focus was eternity. He wanted to bring as many there with him by preaching the gospel of Christ. Let us do the same in our days! May we also be faithful even unto death that we may receive the crown of life given to those that overcome.

FOR FURTHER DISCUSSION

Read Acts 26:19–23.

- Why did the Jewish unbelievers try to murder Paul?

- In what ways did Paul "obtain help from God?" (verse 22)

- How was Paul's witness impacted by the death attempts made against his life?

- In what ways can we obtain the help of God in witnessing for the gospel of Christ during days of increasing persecution?

THE POWER OF AN
INDESTRUCTIBLE LIFE

The Acts of the Apostles provides the family history of Jesus' early disciples. The church has now grown and spread to all areas of the world. We can be thankful for the Jewish apostles who brought the gospel into Gentile contexts.

Christ's church faces persecution today as it has for the past 2,000 years. As noted in the Introduction, it is the Lord Jesus in the church who is being persecuted. Likewise, it is the life of Jesus in the church that has kept it from being destroyed. Jesus embodies the life of God, which is indestructible. We find this gem of a principle in the book of Hebrews:

> *For it is evident that our Lord was descended from Judah, a tribe with reference to which Moses said nothing concerning priests. And this is clearer still, if another priest arises according to the likeness of Melchizedek, who has become a priest not on the basis of a law of physical requirement, but according to* the power of an indestructible life." —Hebrews 7:14–16, emphasis added

This "power of an indestructible life" within Jesus caused him to rise from the dead. Death had no hold over him. Jesus is the high priest whose blood intercedes for us. That blood has wonder-working power. It cannot fail. Church buildings may be destroyed. The flesh of believers may be temporarily snuffed out through martyrdom, while they await a glorious resurrection. Yet, the life of Jesus within the heart of believers cannot be destroyed. That life is indestructible. It is the only power, seen or unseen, which is truly indestructible. Since we are joined to Christ who possesses the indestructible life, we need not be afraid. Fear not!

The life of Jesus empowers the church to stand in times of persecution. The Lion of the Tribe of Judah is roaring. Demons tremble. And the grace of the Lord Jesus Christ is empowering the church now, as it ever has.

Persecution Cannot Separate Us from the Love of God

Because the power of the indestructible life of Jesus forms part of the church's DNA, Jesus can never be taken from the church. Therefore, persecution cannot separate us from the love of God. Brother Paul writes this encouraging message to the church:

> *Who will separate us from the love of Christ? Will tribulation, or trouble, or persecution, or famine, or nakedness, or danger, or sword? Just as it is written: "FOR YOUR SAKE WE ARE KILLED ALL DAY LONG; WE WERE REGARDED AS SHEEP TO BE SLAUGHTERED." But in all these things we overwhelmingly conquer through Him who loved us. For I am convinced that neither death, nor life, nor angels, nor principalities, nor things*

present, nor things to come, nor powers, nor height, nor depth, nor any other created thing will be able to separate us from the love of God that is in Christ Jesus our Lord. —Romans 8:35–39

The love of God is so precious, so boundless and so deep, that even persecution cannot separate us from that love. Neither can demonic powers separate us from the love of God. Instead, we overwhelmingly conquer through Christ who loves us. That is the testimony of the early church in Acts. That is the church's testimony today, even as dark clouds of persecution gather.

As the end of time draws closer, it is likely persecution of the church will increase. Christians need not be governed by fear but we must remain alert. Most importantly, we should continue following the early church's example of worshipping Jesus and witnessing unto him. Be of good cheer, brothers and sisters. Jesus has overcome the world. Through him, we are overcomers too.

ACKNOWLEDGMENTS

I earlier envisioned Muslim-background Christians as being the audience for this book. However, as persecution has mounted against the church globally, I broadened the focus to the general Christian reader.

I would like to thank my dear wife Annette for her encouragement in this project, as well as for editing and proofreading the manuscript. I also appreciate my colleagues Duane A. Miller and Mark Durie for their editorial recommendations.

I have had the privilege of taking two classes on the Acts of the Apostles. The first was taught by Judy Hays Wilkie at Elim Bible Institute and College over 30 years ago. In 2011, I also took a class on Acts taught by Wheaton College's Robert Gallagher, at Assemblies of God Theological Seminary. The love for Acts exhibited by these two instructors proved contagious among their students.

Naturally, I stand responsible for any shortcomings in this publication.

ENDNOTES

1. dictionary.cambridge.org/us/dictionary/english/persecution
2. Fernando, Ajith. Acts (NIVAC). Grand Rapids: Zondervan, 1998, p. 154.
3. blueletterbible.org/lang/lexicon/lexicon.cfm?Strongs=G5512&t=NASB20
4. Gallagher, Robert L. "Hope in the Midst of Trial," in Gallagher, Robert L. and Paul Hertig, eds. Mission in Acts: Ancient Narratives in Contemporary Context. American Society of Missiology Series, No. 34. Maryknoll: Orbis Books, 2004 (4th printing, August 2007), pp. 157–66.
5. Tari, Mel. Like a Mighty Wind. Lake Mary, FL: Creation House, 1971.
6. https://www.blueletterbible.org/study/misc/quotes02.cfm
7. https://www.blueletterbible.org/study/misc/quotes02.cfm
8. https://www.today.com/pets/woman-flies-american-airlines-service-miniature-horse-t161698
9. Meral, Ziya. No Place to Call Home: Experiences of Apostates from Islam, Failures of the International Community. New Malden, Surrey, UK: Christian Solidarity Worldwide, 2008.

10. https://www.youtube.com/watch?v=jJ4sDk4LkAM&list=PLP
    0lSOp9RORx7W0REI8SVK2CNIrMjhS_T&index=10
    (especially 5:54–12:26)

11. "Pastor Brunson Predicts Intensified Persecution of U.S.
    Christians." December 11, 2020. https://www.youtube.com/
    watch?v=teBUjhLlqhs